SWORDFISH PATROL

GEORGE E SADLER

WREXHAM

First published in Wales in 1996
by
Bridge Books
61 Park Avenue
Wrexham
LL12 7AW

ISBN 1-872424-53-8

A CIP catalogue entry for this book
is available from the British Library

Printed and bound by
MFP, Stretford, Manchester

Dedication

To those of my shipmates who did not survive to victory and to my girl friend Dorothy, now fifty years my dear wife, who encouraged me to keep writing when I faltered.

Preface

The realisation that the Second World War was over fifty years ago prompts a stirring of memories and emotions in those of us who were involved. Companionship; loneliness; bravado; fear; joy; sorrow; success; failure; imagination; stupidity; all unfold like the book of Ecclesiastes, except that these sentiments seem to have been contained in an inseparable amalgam of one time. Enrolment in HM Forces offered little choice. Square pegs were shoved unthinkingly into round holes. They did not fit.

This story is of my personal experiences during the War. The flying episodes described are culled from my certified log books, which were signed monthly by the Commanding Officer.

I tell life as I saw it, my point of view, veracious, but related with perhaps a touch of levity, an ingredient without which life might well have proved more difficult.

I enjoyed my service in the Fleet Air Arm. It was both a valuable experience and a growing up for me — an accelerated maturity.

George E Sadler
1996

Contents

The author in flying kit. Note the monogrammed Irvine jacket.

Chapter 1 — War

The outbreak of war found me employed as a sorting clerk in the Head Post Office in Manchester. Having won a scholarship to the local grammar school, then being withdrawn before taking matriculation due to difficult domestic finances, I was aiming to become an Officer of Customs & Excise by working my way through internal Civil Service examinations. It was a hard slog and the working hours were unsociable.

All examinations ceased as we were put on to a war footing. I heaved my books to one side and decided to volunteer. By the Post Office edict, that meant resigning my job. My father, having experienced unemployment following being wounded and gassed in World War 1, spoke strongly against his only offspring giving up his security. I therefore held off, joined the LDV, was provided with an ill fitting uniform and allocated duties guarding the Post Office. This was of course in off duty hours. It was uneventful. The only excitement I can recall was when one member of our platoon shot the Spring Gardens Post Office clock when demonstrating to his relief guard how to operate the safety catch on his rifle.

The forfeiture of job should one volunteer was lifted, so I applied to join the Navy as a telegraphist. None of my family had been connected with seafaring. I wondered why I should, without hesitation, elect to go into the Navy. Was it my being turned out in a sailor suit as an infant? I think not. After consideration, I came to the conclusion that the descriptions I had been given of privations experienced in the trenches made me resolve to eschew Army service. I hadn't given much thought to that unpredictable element, the sea.

There was a long wait. The Navy being the smallest service, albeit the Senior Service, had more applicants than places.

My date for compulsory registration came and went. I still waited. Then my plans changed.

A post office colleague told me, almost with an air of conceit, that he had been successful in gaining a place to train as a pilot in the Fleet Air Arm, as an officer cadet at that. Although he had advanced his scholastic qualifications beyond mine, I felt that I had sufficient ability to do as well as he. Besides, I was getting tired of waiting for my call up. I obtained the necessary forms, sought the required references, made an application to the Royal Navy to train as a naval airman and hoped. To my delight I was called for interview at HMS *St Vincent*, Gosport. We were by now a year into the war. I made myself as smart as I could and set out on the adventure destined to change my life and enable me to make my own way, free from the claustrophobic atmosphere engendered by my over possessive parents. Also, instead of helplessly suffering the frustration of being on the receiving end of German air attacks, I felt I would be able to play my part in taking the war to them.

"I wondered how long you were going to hold it", said the M O. Being over anxious, concerned that I should pass my medical with flying colours, aware that failure to do so would destroy any prospects of becoming a naval airman, I had held the column of mercury steady until I was ready to burst. It had to be maintained at a specific level for one minute by exerting pressure through a tube by mouth. There was no clock. I had no concept of time. When the column of mercury eventually wavered, I reluctantly gave up. "Two minutes ten seconds", said the M O, expressing his surprise. Relieved, I did my best to assume my normal complexion, recover my voice and behave naturally. The other aspects of the medical demanded no further exertions on my part and I was given to understand by the MO's lack of questions and his general air of contentment that my health was satisfactory. So far as he was concerned, I was in.

There was the interview.

To a young man whose total experience of being away from the influence of home was a week's holiday at Cunninghams Young Mens Holiday Camp in the Isle of Man and a walking YHA holiday in the Lake District with pals, the interview came as a shock.

I was guided into a chair on one side of a massive table. The other side accommodated five naval officers resplendent with gold braid who in turn asked me some wide ranging questions. I cannot recall them all, but I remember getting into a confused state over some navigational queries. My reading up of the subject in anticipation of it being raised had obviously been inadequate and I got things hopelessly wrong. The senior officer of the panel, a Commodore, somewhat exasperated at my inability to solve what was to him a simple question about wind vectors, rose and came round to my side of the table. He manipulated a navigational gadget and, adopting an avuncular manner, took time to reveal its mysteries to me. He was delighted when I managed, with some difficulty, to get things right. So was I, because I was getting into a lather.

Emerging somewhat limply from the ordeal I joined the other aspirants and, after an excruciating delay, was told that I had been offered a place on a pilots course. Just what I had hoped for. Following the navigation question I was not surprised that I was not destined to become an observer. I counted myself lucky because less than half of those presenting themselves for interview were accepted and I seemed to be the one least endowed with qualifications.

Another wait. Life was full of waiting. Then, at last, in the bitterly cold February of '41, I was enlisted.

My first experience of service life was at HMS *St Vincent*, Gosport where I had been interviewed. I arrived on a dark cold night and was led by a petty officer across a huge parade ground into a large, severe, brick built block, up two flights of stone stairs and allocated a bunk, the lower of a two tier contraption and a very small locker. The immediate impact on me was the lack of privacy. The floor was crowded with beds with precious little space between. The ablutions on the half landing were rudimentary and cramped. I had certainly got away from home.

CHAPTER 2 — METAMORPHOSIS

The following day the emergence from civilian to service life commenced. We were kitted out. What a transformation!

Jersey, blouse, bell bottoms, boots, underwear, socks, towels, soap, collar, cap, capbox, silk, lanyard, open razor, hussif, greatcoat, knife, oilskin, a kitbag to contain them and Volumes 1 and 2 of the Manual of Seamanship were dispensed at the double. The last items decreed among other fascinating gems of information how ones gear should be cared for and how it should be presented for inspection.

We divested ourselves of civvies and donned our new sailor suits. There were difficulties. Bell bottoms were designed with a drop down 'barn door' front instead of a familiar fly, giving rise to unaccustomed contortions at the heads. The 'heads'? Sorry, we were now aboard ship. The 'heads' were the toilets. Bell bottoms had a small fob pocket under the front flap, but no others at all. No side or hip pockets featured. Obviously the Navy disapproved of hands in pockets.

The blouse, of blue serge like the trousers, was without fastenings and was pulled on over the head. It fitted snugly at the waist and had reveres which widened from the opening at the midriff to the shoulders and terminated as a rectangular collar at the back. In the left revere was a slanting pocket which, having no means of fastening, decanted its contents if one leant forward incautiously.

The blue and white collar, which overlaid the blouse collar, was secured by a tape round ones diaphragm beneath the blouse. It rucked up if one assumed a greatcoat. We learned that this was overcome by inserting ones forearms into the sleeves and swinging the greatcoat over ones head. Another method, should there be a cooperative lady to assist, was to request that she put her arms round you and that she hold the corners of the collar down whilst you put on your coat in a normal manner. This pleasing technique we learned to adopt much later. We new recruits were a harmonious and helpful group and all assisted with advice on how to become acclimatised with our Nelsonian uniforms. Oh yes, they were steeped in history. Naturally as trainee naval airmen we needed bell bottoms, cut so that they could the more easily rolled up when we were swabbing decks. The seamanship manual gave guidance on folding them for storing in a kitbag — in seven folds for the seven seas. We were aboard.

The issue of an identity disc and pay book confirmed it.

As with seamen, the course was split into two watches. We were ordinary seamen. I was starboard watch then further into Forecastle, one of the four parts of the ship. My number was FX85126. In harbour as HMS *St Vincent* was quite properly deemed to be, port and starboard watches were on duty on alternate days after lectures. Over age twenty one was allowed overnight leave if not on duty. If one wanted to 'go ashore' during off duty hours it was essential to go by 'liberty boat'. That meant parading to the specific time of the boat and being subjected to inspection before leaving.

In two to three months we had covered a wide range of subjects through lectures and practical work.

Morning brought a rude and early awakening, a quick wash and shave in very cramped facilities then breakfast. The large dimly lit mess with its grease ingrained tables was the appropriate setting for the food provided, which was poor. Duty orderlies for each table collected unappetizing food from the galley. I cannot remember any item of food over which we rejoiced.

I do remember an early example of the outcome of making a complaint. One morning the Officer of the Day, an RN Lieutenant Commander appeared and asked, "Are there any complaints?" To his surprise, though he hardly showed it, a couple of our crew on the mess deck said "Yes" and produced something to which they objected and with good cause. It was a portion of finnan haddock, a common enough offering at breakfast. This one was revolting. It had a greenish luminescence about it and its smell gave notice of its condition. The Officer of the Day surveyed it. "Have you got a knife and fork?" he asked. Both were provided. He promptly sat to the table and ate it. "Delicious" he said, rose and departed leaving all who witnessed the occurrence open mouthed. I can recall no further complaints.

Breakfast over, the daily routine was divisions. Cadets remained beneath the cloister of the main deck (woe to him who allowed so much as a hand to show), a bugle call, the markers sprinted to their positions, a second call and the whole crew ran to fall in by their divisional markers. Control of the parade ground was under the massive figure of a Major Royal Marines. Strict he was. Looked like General de Gaulle but twice as big. There was drill, then we broke to our separate platoons and marched to lectures under the command of a different member of the group each day.

The personality that cemented itself in the memory of all trainees at *St Vincent* was that of CPO Willmot. His colourful phrases such as "Get fell in, them what's keen get fell in previous" will never be forgotten. His expressed opinion of each course, delivered with panache, was far from complimentary yet we loved him dearly.

Sunday Divisions and church took up the whole of the morning. A raised dais, Captain, Chaplain, marine band on some days, marching and general drill kept us on our toes.

I recall a frigid February morning, frosty, clear and sunny, with an atmosphere in which one could hear a pin drop. We marched to the strains of *Wings over the Navy* feeling mighty proud, though we'd hardly started on our course, and formed a splendid parade before the Captain. He stood resplendent facing us. I was impressed. Behind the assembled ranks something attracted his attention. Unbelievably, it was a British workman, his cord trousers tied with string below the knee, shambling diagonally across our massive parade ground, a shovel sloped over his shoulder.

The Captain, who until then I had regarded as an officer and a gentleman, addressed the offender in stentorian tones, which I vow could be heard beyond Fareham harbour. I'll not reveal what he said, but I was shocked and the Chaplain paled. Yet, I could not but admire his free flowing delivery. I had not experienced such a prelude to a church service. First impressions are not always reliable.

Of course the workman took no notice, no doubt presuming that the outburst was part of the Sunday morning parade routine.

Avoidance of Sunday Divisions was achieved by being Catholic or Non Conformist. Those professing such convictions were permitted to go ashore, presumably to their designated places of worship, though I doubted the veracity of some escapees. Almost all of our signing on forms bore the legend 'C of E' as standard, which put a stop to a quiet Sunday morning.

Our instruction occupied each day from divisions until five o'clock, mid way through the first dog watch; until noon, the end of the forenoon watch, on Saturday and Sunday. We broke for a midday meal, the only substantial meal of the day. The evening meal consisted of bread and jam and tea.

Considering we were at *St Vincent* but something like two and a half months the subjects we studied were wide ranging. In that relatively short time we were introduced to seamanship with some detail on knots, anchors, boat pulling in Shoreham Harbour, gunnery, target practice at icy wind swept Stokes Bay range, morse, semaphore, flag recognition, signalling, much drill and the mysteries of the progress of a new recruits career in the Royal Navy.

Of course we had volunteered to be naval airmen so we were lectured on airmanship, theory of flight and navigation. We learned that a north wind blew from the north, whereas a northerly current flowed to the north and that miles an hour could be forgotten in favour of knots.

I fancy there were odd periods of 'make and mend', when we could address ourselves to our uniforms, 'boning' shoe toecaps until they resembled mirrors and discovering by experiment how to wash a collar without the blue running into the white, yet softening the dark navy to a lighter blue to suggest one was not a 'sprog'. The establishment found time for us to drag out the very heavy refectory tables from the mess deck and scrub them clean, a somewhat fruitless exercise without decent cleaning materials. I recall, against orders, sneaking off during such sessions and resorting to a seasoned old salt in the recesses of the barracks, who served as barber and who could give splendid guidance on many nautical matters, including how to roll tobacco. Haircuts had to be very short. If they were not so, a stubby forefinger in the back as one paraded for inspection before going ashore, signified that your intended shore leave was off. I can't recall how one was meant to get ones hair cut apart from using the clandestine method I adopted.

We were divided into two watches. Every other night we were on duty parading at eight o'clock, the first watch. On such nights we did not see our bunks. Duties varied dependent upon the exigencies of the day. During the period I spent at *St Vincent* there was much enemy night bombing; so one might be on a pick and shovel party or be in the vicinity of the oil installations disposing of the common incendiary bombs. We were employed on unpleasant tasks in the blackout and got virtually no sleep before returning hollow eyed to base shortly before breakfast. My first night in uniform I spent balanced precariously on the running board of a trailer fire pump in a failed attempt to get a little sleep.

There was a serious side to all this. It became apparent to us that there were more cadets on the course than there were places at flying school. The cadets were not pressed men. They had volunteered. Hence, there was competition. There were exams to be faced. A good result was essential. There was need to study.

Doing a bit of swotting was difficult. Lighting in our sleeping quarters was virtually non existent and on the mess deck it equated to a Toc H lamp. If one stayed in on off duty nights it was asking for trouble. An emergency and you were roped in without ceremony and without sleep.

Going ashore overnight was one solution, if one could find a bed in the YMCA or a similar establishment amid the bomb devastation of Portsmouth, but one had to take care. During the day we wore working rig. To catch the first liberty boat one had to be in full uniform within five minutes and forego tea. The next boat was at 7pm, which was a difficult time to get out.

It was a disturbing revelation to discover how easy it was to fall foul of thieving hands and find that waking up in the morning ashore you had no collar, or no silk, or indeed no cap! One had almost to chain things on and that elusive sleep became a cat nap. 'Things was 'ard but we was learning'. Lost gear meant trouble on inspection and the cost of replacement of missing items.

We did get out to occasional dances on a Saturday. Cosham was a favourite place but the transport to and fro was unpredictable and there was many a scramble to return to *St Vincent* on time.

I managed to get on to the *St Vincent* soccer team for a match against HMS *Collingwood* at Eastleigh one Saturday afternoon. That was near disaster. During the match I seized up with severe pain in my thigh. I could barely walk. On my return there were searching inquiries as to why I was unable to march and much expressed unbelief, before I was permitted to report sick. That was at the end of the working day, having been given permission to make my own hobbling way to and from lectures. I was kept in the sick bay and given alternate scalding hot and icy cold compresses and advised that I had burst a blood vessel. To my great concern I was still in the sick bay when the examinations started. Fortunately I was isolated from the others and allowed to sit those I had missed on my own, under careful supervision — an odd experience. On consideration, I suppose it was quite a concession for me to be permitted to take two thirds of the examinations with the rest of the course — that portion not having been sat before my discharge and to take the other third by myself with a personal invigilator. What a sweat!

There was the inevitable tenseness of awaiting results.

I was through and learned that I was to proceed to Elmdon where I would commence my flying instruction. Sadly, the pleasant fellow who shared my double deck bunk, with whom I had become quite friendly, did not make it. We bid each other a fond goodbye. Being keen on qualifying as flying crew he told me he was going to try the RAF.

CHAPTER 3 — AERIAL ASPIRATIONS

What a change was Elmdon. In 1941 it was a grass aerodrome. The terminal building, constructed in the '30s International style of architecture, with metal framed windows, curved brickwork and flat roof, imagined itself to be a warship, presumably in deference to trainee naval airmen, for it was painted over in camouflage browns and greens. It served as dormitory, mess, lounge, and offices. Compared to *St Vincent* it was a rest home.

We were there to undergo a course of elementary flying in Tiger Moth aircraft, De Haviland 82a. Our instructors were RAF personnel. Gone were the drills and divisions. Gone were the watch and watch about duties. We could go out in the evenings without hindrance unless some unusual duty or emergency arose. Unlike Gosport, there was mercifully negligible German bombing during our stay and longer hours of daylight, so our course was uninterrupted. We enjoyed the food served by civilian caterers instead of having to serve as mess orderlies. Moreover, we were better off. We received flying pay. Our object was to learn to fly and virtually nothing else.

The 'virtually nothing else' was a mite upset by the Senior Naval Officer. He was a shadowy figure who never deigned to appear, but his influence was there nonetheless. When a new course arrived at Elmdon one of the first moves was to have a group photograph taken. The SNO had one delivered to him at once. It was pinned on the wall in his private quarters with names appended so that he could readily identify individuals and he did! With firm deliberation he ringed the heads of four members of each course. They were designated 'Squad Leaders'.

As one might guess, my head was one of them.

The duties accruing to a Squad leader were not irksome. I can scarcely remember what they were, excepting for collecting laundry money. It became more difficult and troublesome when, on occasions, an assembly of cadets behaved boisterously and not in accordance with course requirements. The sudden appearance of a course officer enquiring angrily what was going on and why and who was in charge was enough to upset a Squad leader's equilibrium. Being 'in charge' of a group, yet being of the same rank and seniority and not having authority to put anybody on a charge, was not unalloyed joy. It caused one to preach and cajole which did nothing to boost ones popularity with course colleagues. The complaining officer was not over impressed either. My predecessor on the overlapping course was a huge chunk of Canadian the size of a barn door. His whispered commands were dutifully observed by his peers. My ten stone six presence did not have the same effect, though I did profit to a degree because we both rejoiced in the name 'George'. That designation carried some respect.

Being required to report to the Senior Naval Officer shortly after my arrival on the station, with alarm bells ringing that some damning report must have accompanied me from *St Vincent* was alarming. I was relieved that the summons was to land me with an unlooked-for responsibility and nothing further. The SNO being a strict disciplinarian, I was relieved that I had no cause to appear before him again.

The course members at Elmdon, Number 14 EFTS, included RAF trainees. Some of them, older than the average course age, were destined to become flying instructors and consequently would never become operational pilots. Whilst the majority accepted the arrangements, some were chagrined about it. This disappointment I recall being expressed in a bit of doggerel entitled *The Flying Instructor's Lament,*

> What did you do in the War Daddy?
> How did you help us to win?
> Circuits and bumps and turns Laddie,
> And how to get out of a spin.
> Woe and alack and misery me,
> I trundle around in the sky.
> Instead of machine gunning Nazis,
> I'm teaching young hopefuls to fly

There was much flying to be done other than with operational squadrons, both in the Navy and RAF, but we aspired to be first line pilots. I understand the feelings of those directed into other fields. My flying instructor on the intermediate flying course, an RAF Flying Officer (F/O), was much frustrated teaching trainees after having been employed on more exciting duties. He rejoiced on being posted back to an operational squadron. We celebrated with him on the strength of it. He proved his point later when flying a Beaufighter, by disposing of three Heinkel 111's. But that's another story.

We started with some preliminary classroom work and reading of manuals so that we understood, or said we did, the principles of flight, the petrol and ignition system of the Tiger Moth, the strict instructions relating to airscrew swinging drill on starting up the engine and the sequence of our flying course itinerary. We were kitted for flying with Sidcot, a one piece gabardine flying suit arrayed with zips, helmet, goggles and other requirements, shown how to wear and use a parachute and allocated to our flying instructors. Mine was Sergeant Jameson, a large imposing taciturn character.

Arrayed in my aeronautical gear, feeling apprehensive and no doubt looking a complete 'sprog', I reported to the Sergeant for my first flight. To my discomfort, I found that I was in the rear cockpit behind Jameson's solid person so that I could see naught ahead. We got airborne after some preliminaries and did some general flying during which the aircraft was put through its paces, excluding anything fancy like aerobatics. After a few minutes, Jameson addressed me through the communicating Gosport tube. He got no reply. He tried again. Still no reply. He twisted round to confirm that his passenger was still aboard and discovered that I had my head down over the side being violently sick. His taciturnity evaporated. He was disgusted. My first twenty five minutes 'Cockpit Layout and Air Experience' adventure was not promising. I descended to terra firma from the Tiger Moth, when we had landed, a pale shade of grey and steered an uncertain course for the Squadron Office, my parachute bumping behind me.

I know not if Sergeant Jameson repaired to the bar and had a stiff drink or two to recover his composure, but recover it he did. He persevered with his sickly bell bottomed trainee naval airman pupil. I was introduced to straight and level flying, taxying without depositing the aircraft on its nose, climbing, gliding, stalling, taking off into wind and gliding approach and landing. Having familiarised myself with the foregoing with varying degrees of success, the instructor demonstrated how to cause the aircraft to go into a spin, which was alarming and how to recover from a spin before burying the machine in the ground, which was illuminating and comforting. Rounding things off with directions of what to do in the event of fire and how to abandon the aircraft in an emergency — these last to fill one with confidence, he adjudged me to be fit, possibly, to fly solo. I therefore had to fly with another instructor who would assess my prowess and, if satisfied, would give me the 'thumbs up' signal.

He did so. On 6th May '41, after ten hours of dual instruction, I was allowed to go off on my own. Some of the fellows went solo in eight hours, so that once I had exceeded eight myself I was getting anxious. If one was not considered competent after twelve hours it was bad news.

Once off on one's own it felt more free and one could progress to instrument flying, aerobatics, forced landing practice and some air navigation. I began to enjoy the course. We had some compulsory Link Trainer sessions. I don't think anybody cared for them because it seemed so removed from the real thing. I did ask if I might make a parachute jump, but was given a very firm "no". "We're meant to get you trained. Suppose you broke an ankle on landing. You'd be off the course", was the response from the Commanding Officer.

In the seven weeks between 21st April and 11th June I had done 65 hours flying and 6 hours Link Trainer and had satisfactorily finished the course. With the other successful trainees I was cleared to go forward to Intermediate Flying School. An unexpected bonus was that, having been a squad leader, I was given the choice either of going to Canada or staying in the UK. I chose the former.

My final move I regretted. I decided to be a sociable squad leader, joining the celebration tipple at the Barley Mow at Sheldon. I was not abstemious but temperate. All went well until somebody slipped me a mickey finn. I was very quickly exceedingly ill. I recall seeing the pool outside the pub with a squadron of white banded sailors caps floating around in it when we were ejected from the establishment. I remembered little else and was grateful that one of my close friends managed to walk me back, quite a considerable distance, to Elmdon. The following morning I was still in a bad state with a raging headache. It took more than twenty four hours before I began to recover. Giving somebody a doped drink is a rotten trick and highly dangerous.

We, those going to Canada, enjoyed a pleasant break. The weather was glorious as it should be in June, in England. Awaiting embarkation, which proved to be from Liverpool, we were guests of the RAF Station at Wilmslow south of Manchester, we did naught but laze in the sunshine and accept the best the cookhouse could offer, which was not much. We must have remained there for all of three weeks.

Our next move was not so pleasant. The basically appointed troopship, *Northumberland* was a wretched vessel so overloaded with troops that swinging hammocks was not feasible. The decks were littered with bodies overnight. I can confidently assert that the food was the worst experienced during the whole of my naval service. We proceeded on our zig zagging anti submarine course to Canada in very different weather from that at balmy Wilmslow. After eleven miserable days, we disembarked at Halifax, Nova Scotia. From there, after having a feast of ham and eggs at a restaurant by courtesy of our accompanying officer who somehow arranged for us a monetary dollar advance, we entrained on the Canadian National Railway. It was an overnight haul to Kingston. Progress was at an unhurried rate with occasional unscheduled stops, but the journey was punctuated with forays to the dining car for sumptuous meals. It was diametrically opposed to our shipboard experience in both comfort and culinary contributions.

Collins Bay, about seven miles from Kingston on the bank of Lake Ontario, was reached by road through an unbuilt area in which the principal features were the penitentiary and a lofty grain elevator. It was the site of the Canadian Air Force Station, 31 Service Flying Training School. It was to be our home for our intermediate and advanced flying training.

The weather was scorching hot. We were accommodated in huts, about fifty to each I would think and settled in. There were duck boards outside and I questioned their purpose but found out when eventually we had some rain. On the day of our arrival, friends on the preceding course showed us the ropes. A bus came to the camp after flying was over for the day. I was off with them to be introduced to Kingston. It was a dime in the box on the bus, no change given, for any distance to Kingston.

Returning was different. It was a pitch black moonless night.

There was no twilight in Canada. Once the sun set, night came down abruptly like a shutter. The only transport was by taxi — Ford V8s they were, and we clubbed together for the fare, getting as many aboard as the cabby would allow. As it happened, I was in the front seat alongside the driver. Something around seventy miles an hour appeared to be the going rate with headlights full on and the high powered well sprung vehicle flying over the indifferent road surface. A taxi returning to Kingston approached us at a similar speed, headlights full beam, no dipping. The closing rate was alarming. As the other vehicle bore down upon us I closed my eyes. I felt sure that I would not open them again. I was terrified. The two cabs crossed without mishap to my unbelief. Miraculously I had survived my first day in the Province. I had also learned that night shades fell with a clatter and that in Canada one drove on the right!

The flying school 31 SFTS was quite large and stood by the north shore of Lake Ontario. It was flat, as indeed is the whole of South Ontario and, unlike Elmdon, had runways. Whilst there was a Senior Naval Officer as at the elementary training school, our instruction was entirely through RAF personnel. Within our naval group, authority was vested in the senior naval non commissioned officer for general discipline and duties. The three naval officers transferring from other persuasions to flying training with us, we saw little of, apart from during our flying instruction. They were housed, no doubt more comfortably in the officers quarters which were remote from our congested hut.

The atmosphere differed from the UK. The weather was gloriously hot and sunny. There was light as opposed to blackout, no air raids and no reason why we should not advance our flying abilities without let or hindrance. We were lucky with the aircraft, brand new Harvard IIs. Previous courses had laboured with Fairey Battles which were elderly, heavy and underpowered. From what I observed they took a considerable amount of runway to get airborne. Out of sight they were before they got unstuck. Twenty Two course, ours, must have made quite an impression on the local populace, because the rasping note of the Harvards was strident compared to the dull drone of the Battles. They were smart, painted bright yellow without a dent or a scratch on them — before we started flying!

Additional to we embryo naval airmen, the course was made up by RAF trainees thirteen of whom had reached Canada by travelling East across the Pacific from Malaya where they had been planting rubber. A handsome well educated crew they were.

I was allocated to B flight and to my instructor, F/O Beaumont. To my pleasure, Alan Hodgson, a Yorkshire boy from Whitby was under the same instructor. We formed a close friendship he and I. In appearance we differed greatly he being as dark as I was fair.

The intermediate course ran for about six weeks. It consisted of practical flying, study in lecture rooms on the principles of flight, meteorology, navigation, use of

The author (5th from right second row from the back) and the other members of his course at 31 Service Flying Training School, Kingston, Ontario, 1941.

instruments and kindred subjects — and Link Trainer sessions. The last was our personal responsibility and was by arrangement between each trainee and the Link Trainer officer. He kept a careful log of our hours with him. We'd got to put the time in on that aspect of instrument flying training or lose some privileges. Six days shalt thou labour was the rule following the good book and it alternated twixt Christian and Jew in that we had Sunday off one week and Saturday off the next. Hours of daylight were long and flying was spread over the day. If not flying, nor at lectures it was sometimes possible to steal outside the confines of the station and enjoy a dip in the lake. This diversion was in strong competition with Link Trainer sessions and the weather was scorching.

The Harvard was a fine sophisticated aircraft with instrumentation one might find in an operational plane — quite a complicated cockpit as compared to the Tiger Moth. My instructors at Elmdon seemed disappointed that I had not the experience of driving a motor vehicle, not even a motor cycle, so that the comparisons they drew between handling powered vehicles on land and in the air were meaningless. My personal mode of transport was a pedal cycle. I surveyed the complex instrument layout, drew a deep breath and tried to absorb it. I took heart, noting that other members of the course were rendered thoughtful and remembered that I had flown solo.

There was need to learn the cockpit layout, understand the use of the instruments and read mark and learn the manual on the aircraft before getting airborne. A familiarisation flight, this time in an enclosed cockpit, some dual flying with the instructor, a solo flight check, a confirmation that I could recite the mnemonic which ensured that procedures for starting up, taking off and landing were strictly observed and never forgotten. There were flaps to control, an undercarriage to retract or lower, a pitch control to operate and flight and engine instruments to acquaint me with the performance of the craft. Instructor and check instructor in agreement, I was permitted to fly solo. It was at first a dodgy business taxying the aircraft to the take off position. The foot controls operated the rudder and, if one depressed the forward part of the pedals, the brakes. They were very sensitive and operated separately one each wheel. An oleo leg could be strained by a too enthusiastic use of them causing a ground loop.

Airborne, solo, in a spanking new Harvard was both a thrill and an anxiety. Once one had gained a familiarity with the controls and the feel of things, it became a pleasure, and there was a desire to get in the air more frequently than was possible. After all, others had to fly too.

Twenty two course proceeded to a strict pattern. Example by the instructor in dual flying running to fifty two hours interlarded with twenty three hours solo flying practising what we had been taught. We covered straight and level flight, spinning and recovery, powered approach and landing, glide approach and landing, forced landing, low flying, side slipping, aerobatics, instrument flying, instrument take off, steep and climbing turns and simple pilot navigation.

The essential necessity of familiarity with the controls was sharply brought to testing point by another kind of flying — night flying. I found the prospect frightening.

Until this arose I could see what I was doing good or bad, right or wrong. On the moonless night programmed for this new adventure I could see naught.

The smoky flares illuminating the runway giving uneven patches of light and darkness, the reliance on instruments, which with the restricted cockpit lighting were not easy to read and the confusing reflections from the perspex canopy made the outlook obscure to me. Two and a half hours much needed guidance from my instructor and I was adjudged to be competent to try it on my own.

As I lined up nervously, adrenaline pumping, with the marker flares, obviously not quite into wind according to the direction the smoke was being blown, my mind went back to the hymn I had often sung as a chorister. *Lead Kindly Light* — "I was not ever thus nor prayed that thou should lead me on. I loved to choose and see my path but now lead thou me on". The prayer was unspoken but emotionally felt. It was answered.

Along the flaming flight path, gathering speed, then lift off into the night sky and out over the lake. Now was the time to appreciate the true value of the aircraft's instruments. Was the plane level? At what altitude was I flying? Was my course correct? Was the correct angle being achieved as I banked and turned? After a brief period gaining confidence came the next problem. How to get down safely? First get into the right position and height downwind of the runway. Look out for other aircraft. Make sure it was signalled that I was clear to land. Another set of questions arose. Was my airspeed right as I approached the flare path? Were the flaps operating? Was the undercarriage down and properly locked? The information was spread out before me. Following the drill worked. Believing the instruments worked. Right. Judge the angle of the flares on approaching and lose height and speed. Level off and achieve the proper height just above the ground to ease back on the throttle and settle to three point landing. Grounded. Good. Steady. Keep the aircraft straight. Gradually come to rest then taxi off the flare path — careful with the brakes. So that was night flying. Putting one's trust and confidence in believing what the flight instruments indicated and realising that one cannot fly by the seat of one's pants in the dark. Another lesson learned. It seemed that Link Trainer had its uses.

Having completed the intermediate course successfully we were granted five days leave. I bid farewell to Flying Officer Beaumont who was to join a fighter squadron. The one disaster of twenty two course was an RAF trainee from UK who lost his life crashing into the lake on his night flying solo. I temporarily lost the company of my friend Alan whose relations resident in the USA drove up to the border at Niagara and entertained him in the USA during the break. It necessitated obtaining civilian clothes and a visa from Ottawa the States not then being at war. I had little money having made an allowance to my parents out of my pay, but got as far as Toronto where, exercising some charm and demonstrating my postal circulation knowledge, I got to enter and inspect the Toronto main post office and was invited out for a meal.

The recess gives opportunity to remember other activities and happenings. The summer was scorching hot and our working uniform was bell bottoms of heavy rough woollen cloth and a white blouse. The former were most uncomfortable and I envied the RAF boys who were issued with khaki shorts. They were neither available nor permitted to us not being uniform. My research through the Seamanship Manual revealed that in hot climes for example the Mediterranean or the Far East, seamen wore shorts, Number 5's I think it was. Somehow I got permission or else assumed it, to buy some white shorts as did Alan and we felt so much better. We had them laundered at a small Chinese establishment in Kingston from whence they emerged brilliant white long before the present soap and detergent manufacturers had discovered the words. In a world of constant change I was delighted to discover the same little Chinese laundry in the same place when I visited Kingston fifty one years later.

Food in the camp was monotonous but satisfactory. An occasional meal out was a pleasant change, the Chinese restaurant being a first class place to go. Should a diner make any small criticism regarding a meal, the entire staff of the place would appear, make obsequious bows and apologies and remedy things. There were no faults to find. I wonder if a complaint would result in the same action today?

One offering from our mess was tomato juice which was thick and tasteless. Gerry Loughlan, one of the ex Malayan group who had inveigled himself onto the canteen committee took pointed objection to it and said so. He assumed the role as an expert on the subject of the quality control, preservation and presentation of tomatoes and held forth from his wide experience in that field. His persistence resulted in a vast improvement so that I reverted to tomato juice and laid off the 'stubby orange' which I had to buy. I wondered how such erudition could result from growing rubber in Malaya. Gerry conceded that he knew damn all about tomatoes, but worked on the hunch that somebody was doing a fiddle and we as a result were being given an inferior product. His determination paid off. He didn't seem to be able to improve anything else.

Another item for round condemnation was tea. In UK people know how to provide a good cup of tea whether they brew, mash or infuse it depending upon the strata of society in which they move. The basic rules though essential are simple — Boiling water, warm the pot, empty it, put in the requisite amount of tea per person — "one spoonful for each person and one for the pot" being pretty standard — take the pot to the kettle, brew, m or i and leave for four minutes. Result — satisfaction. In Canada they have no concept of how to prepare that healing beverage. Tepid water, a cold cup, a tea bag on a string and a spoon to agitate the resultant indifferent fluid was the order of the day. They might as well as nipped down the East coast to Boston, salvaged some of the stuff tipped into the sea and used that! I'm sorry to observe that fifty one years after my first experience they're still at it, even domestically. One cannot obtain a decent cup of tea in what I have seen of Canada.

Folk were hospitable to us in Kingston. Dances were held at the camp some evenings, not exceeding once a week. Girls were brought up by coach and returned home by the same means. They could not come any other way and obviously the arrangements were pretty tight. Friendships were made at the dances which led to invitations to visit families, go out on weiner roasts (picnics) and generally socialise. The girls must have had quite a selection of trainees to choose from as course followed course. Outnumbered as we were by RAF personnel on the station, we naval types had a distinct advantage on scarcity value alone. The bell bottoms and slim midriff were splendidly suited for dancing and the Fleet Air Arm trainee was seldom short of a partner. There were but twenty six of us on the course. It seemed quite a novelty to the young ladies to be clasped discretely and introduced to the slow romantic tempo of the waltz.

We got in some sport. Swimming in the lake was common for those cared for it. There were no facilities, just a very short stretch of narrow stony shore near to the camp entrance sufficed. I recall playing soccer in some special event in Queens University campus and being introduced to rugby. For me that was "hello and goodbye". The Malayan boys were steeped in rugby and were incensed that not one of their number was given a place in the Station team. They therefore challenged the station team to a match. As there were but thirteen of them they sought two more to

The author (standing third from the right) in the 835 Squadron soccer team, HMS *Sparrowhawk*, Hatston, near Kirkwall, summer 1942.

make up a fifteen. Regarding Alan and I as fit physical specimens, they cajoled us into playing. Regrettably they neglected to apprise us of rules. We were soccer players. It was a fierce encounter with no quarter given. It became even more so for me when I had my eye blackened jumping at a line out. That got my dander up and resulted in such commitment that my fair tackle on the Station Sports Officer (I was doing about forty knots at the moment I took him) resulted in his being unable to take any further part in the proceedings. I finished with half a shirt, a black eye and several lacerations. The ex Malayan boys were ecstatic because our hut won.

One illuminating experience I must recount. I was returning from Brockville late one evening following an abortive attempt to call on a friend's Canadian relations, fortunate to pick up a comfortable lift with a business man. We were driving through open country when the heavens opened. The display of the Northern Lights was scintillating. My driver pulled over on to the soft shoulder. We got out of the car and fell silent in awe. We stood under what only I can liken to the interior of a massive pyramid from the apex of which beamed brilliant sparkling lights of many colours — something like a spectrum of infinite size and power. Slowly it drifted away from us and after a little while, we resumed our journey. It was interesting to read the American newspapers the following day. The display was so intense that it literally dimmed the lights of Broadway, New York, some three hundred miles distant!

This happening took our minds off things terrestrial for a spell. That reminds me that I did some liaison work between the Anglian Young Peoples' Association in UK to which I belonged and the branch in Kingston where Rev Kenneth Blachford was the incumbent.

Back to the skies, because flying training was the purpose of our Canadian visit, pleasant though the diversions were. We had a further six weeks on advanced training. Different instructors and a different curriculum made our flying that much more sophisticated. We covered pilot navigation, instrument take off, flapless landing, wind speed direction finding, use of RT, formation flying, more night flying, simulated attacks with camera then with live ammunition, low flying, bombing, dive bombing and of course the ever present Link Trainer stint. Low flying stimulated the urge to fly under the Thousand Islands Bridge over the St Lawrence just East of Lake Ontario, the bridge linking Canada and the USA. It wasn't difficult because the bridge rose high above the river. However, we were strictly warned against any such adventure, the penalty being to be put off course. As the aircraft were clearly marked and recognisable, the warning was heeded.

After about 170 hours flying, dual and solo, the course was completed at the end of October. By then the hot summer had passed, temperatures had fallen and the country was dyed with the flamboyant colours of the Fall. It was the end of a season, the end of our anxious efforts. Flying checks had been conducted by senior instructors, and reports made on our theoretical studies by the tutors. An interminable wait ensued. Inevitably, not all trainees would be successful.

Twenty two course sweated.

The RAF results, passes and failures, were revealed well before ours. There were rejoicings and commiserations. Special congratulations to those who were to be commissioned, with perhaps a touch of envy by the less fortunate. There was also notice of the date of graduation day, the formal presentation of wings.

In the fullness of time, the results for the Senior Service were unveiled. It was done by the posting of a typewritten sheet of paper on our general notice board. It read:-

"The following members of number Twenty Two course are now permitted to wear their flying badge" — signed by the Senior Naval Officer. There was also an indication of those who were to be commissioned.

So that was it. I was thrilled to be on the list and to be successful on both counts.

How proud I would be to wear my wings, even though I had not even reached operational training. Were the wings to be presented? Were they just to be issued? If so when? The answers were neither and never. We had to repair to an enterprising Kingston trader and buy a pair of wings. They were a pale imitation of the real thing because the anchor in the middle of the badge was of woven material not a metal one as in the authentic job. Those of us who were entitled bought them, got busy with our hussifs and wore them.

The RAF graduates attended their grand passing out parade with marching and bands and the presentation and pinning on of wings by the Commanding Officer. Those to be commissioned were directed to remove their badge of rank, replace it with a white flash and thereafter regard themselves as pilot officers.

I think we naval types went out for a drink.

The confirmation that I would be commissioned, albeit after I had returned to a naval establishment in the UK, released my kit bag from containing my naval gear. That meant that once I had stowed the naval items I wished to retain, relatively few, it could be stuffed to the top with whatever I could afford to buy and take home for family and friends in England. There were acute shortages at home, rationing and clothing coupons which strictly limited the number if items one could buy. My entire naval uniform, I determined, would consist of what I stood up in.

The finest establishment for laying in stores in Canada was Eatons. They had an order office in Kingston where one might examine samples of their wide ranging selection of goods available, order them and collect them over a brief period. Of course, I had ordered some items before the results were made known on the assumption that I would return home after the course. There's optimism for you! I'll not list the contents of my kit bag. Suffice it to say that there was something for everybody. My young lady, now some fifty years my wife, probably did as well as anybody. In spite of my limited means I had been frugal and therefore found it necessary to buy a large robust suitcase to contain my loot over and above what the bag would contain.

November '41 found us heading homewards, rail to Halifax, Nova Scotia, a cold and snowy landscape compared to what it was in June, then on a vessel of some quality, *The Warwick Castle*. We took but five days to reach the haven of the Clyde and anchor of Gourock. I should mention the crowning insult we endured compared to the newly commissioned RAF fellows on Twenty Two course. It was decreed that we, being leading seamen by rank and our being at sea, immediately be given duties to perform, whilst the newly promoted cruised comfortably at their ease in first class accommodation. Fortunately the chores we were allocated did not include our acting as cabin stewards, else we might have ventilated our feelings.

The safe transfer ashore of a loaded kit bag and a bulging case without mishap gave me concern, as did the thought of HM Customs.

I was apprehensive that an Officer would discover something attracting duty or indeed be prohibited. No bother. No inspection. We were transferred to the shore safely and directed into a troop train, which was waiting alongside. This was RAF transport, first stop Bournemouth. The fact that we naval types desired to report to Lee on Solent was of no matter. We were on our way, a very small minority of the passengers. Nobody bothered about what we had to say. There was something else we all had to bother about. To cater for the inner man a soup kitchen arrangement had been set up here and there on the train. That was satisfactory though rudimentary. What to bother about then? Well, it was a cold November. The train, of very dilapidated elderly rolling stock, was unheated and there were no toilets in the carriages. At least our conditions equated with the promotees aboard!

Our journey to Bournemouth was uncomfortable and uneventful, but we were back home safe with our small offerings for our loved ones intact. We were able to see some of the war ravaged areas on our journey and realise how fortunate we were to have had a summer holiday away from it all.

Decanted from the train and taken into RAF Bournemouth, the expected happened. The officer to whom we reported questioned why we had come. Explaining was pointless. Apparently it was our fault that we were reporting to the wrong station. He was desirous that we departed out of his area of responsibility and by some irregular means of transport supported by grudgingly provided travel vouchers we eventually reached Lee on the Solent. Lee, HMS *Daedalus*, was the HQ of the Fleet Air Arm. It gave us a sense of belonging, though our stay was but transitory. The brevity of our sojourn was squeezed by the arrival of the crew of the aircraft carrier *Argus*. Bomb damage to the flight deck necessitated her coming in for repairs and the ship's complement were sent ashore to Lee. The paperwork relative to our being commissioned, grants to purchase uniform, train passes for leave and orders as to our reporting for our next course were dispensed with haste so that our unwanted presence did not clutter up the overcrowded station. In quick sticks we were able to get to London, find a naval tailor and outfitter of our choice, kit ourselves out with a smart officer's uniform, black with gold accessories and speed for our homes feeling mighty proud.

An incident just before this splendid transition took place put things into perspective. Along with other bell-bottomed sailors, all in greatcoats against the cold wind, no badges visible, I was standing waiting for a bus. One of our single engined aircraft flew overhead. The lad standing next to me gazed up at it with awe. "Bloody 'ell" he muttered, I turned to him and questioned if I had heard aright. I had. "Bloody 'ell" he ejaculated, this time with more feeling. I asked why he was so concerned. "I wouldn't go up in them" he asserted. "Bloody 'ell". "They're not so bad" I said, feeling my chest swelling on my jersey, with pride or was it conceit? "You wouldn't go up in them?" he queried. "I do" I said. "I'm a pilot". He surveyed me with shocked surprise. "Bloody 'ell" he said. Feeling by now like a proud pouter pigeon, king of the loft, I condescended to enquire of his line of business. "Me", he replied, "I'm in submarines". The swift descent from the air to beneath the sea brought my feet back to earth. The bubble burst. "Bloody hell" I said. This fellow had presumably been doing something. I had it yet to do. Better that, instead of preening myself, I got stuck in to doing my job as best I could, but first with modest step, for some leave.

Chapter 4 — Aspirations almost Achieved

Early December came the great transformation. Regaled in our smart Officers uniforms, the course assembled at The Royal Naval College, Greenwich.

This magnificent establishment, Royal Greenwich from the fifteenth century, beloved by Henry VII, birthplace of Henry VIII and of his daughters Elizabeth and Mary, run down under Cromwell, part restored by Webb for Charles II and gloriously completed by Wren for William III, was to be our home for a fortnight. The four splendid quadrangles with twin domes, perfections of symmetry, had miraculously remained virtually undamaged by enemy action. Only six miles from central London, it was unbelievable. Within this building of generous elegant proportions and lofty ceilings, was the sumptuous painted dining hall. There was also an impressive chapel in which we attended church service. Here Lord Nelson lay in state. Beyond, through magnificent wrought iron gates, a walkway led to the Queen's House built by Inigo Jones. Dull would any young officer be who was not impressed, indeed overawed, with this architectural gem steeped in history.

We formally greeted and congratulated each other, using our new Officers form of address. There was a feeling that we'd had a light hearted and jolly time during our training to date, but now we were ready for the serious business of the Royal Navy at war. We were now naval officers.

About the first impact of our being at Royal Naval College Greenwich was the small matter of dress, something unexpected. At dinner, served in the splendour of the Painted Hall, it was essential that officers wore bow ties — single ended ones. There was a frantic rush of last minute shopping, then the frenetic matter of tying them in limited time twixt the last lecture of the day and dinner. The recourse to a mirror was unhelpful.

For ten months we had no necessity to wrestle with a collar stud, never mind stiff collars and bow ties. Double ended bow ties made sense. The length could be adjusted, but they were out. Out also were any made up substitutes as indeed were their wearers. My grateful thanks went to Andy Stovell who had the dexterity to produce a perfect job and was most generous in his assistance.

Before the fortnight was through we were adept at tying bow ties. We had to be so if we desired dinner and did we not desire it. Service at table was perfection as indeed was the food. I felt some embarrassment in being served such splendid meals, a la carte, whilst the civilian population, I had observed during my leave, was scraping along on very basic rations. The weekly ritual of Captain's Evening was to be savoured. The Painted Hall was the ideal setting for such a banquet, the tables brilliant with silver beneath the richly ornamented ceiling. Domestically, until then, I had little experience of the correct way to pass the port. I learned.

One interesting concession to the Senior Service was revealed at the Loyal Toast. "Gentlemen, the King", did not result in our being upstanding. We remained chairborne. The history behind this procedure went back to the wooden ships, back to Horatio, when to rise without care could result in a damaged cranium, there being so little headroom. The monarch, having discovered this by personal painful experience, made the concession that, when expressing their loyalty, naval officers remain seated. The vast dimensions of the Painted Hall did not merit any change in procedure. Oh no! The concession granted, it was strictly adhered to regardless of

Officers Torpedo Training Course, HMS *Jackdaw*, Crail, winter 1942. Author is 4th from the left, middle row.

where we were. We remained seated.

We had lectures, the details of which I cannot quite recall, a bit on psychology, some very minor duties such as fire fighting patrols and, what all of us will certainly recall, the instruction on unarmed combat by a delightful diminutive mature RN Commander.

The fortnight passed quickly. We became acclimatised to our new status and appreciated the privilege of being naval officers. We also thirsted to know what happened next. What would our drafting be? This was to be the first division of our course — operational training as fighter or torpedo bomber pilots for the fortunate ones.

The news broke. I was to report to RNAS Crail, HMS *Jackdaw*, for a torpedo bomber course just on Christmas.

Rail transport in 1941 was slow and unpredictable. Immediately after Christmas I travelled by train from Manchester to Glasgow to Edinburgh thence to Crail — a long day. I met up with Alan Hodgson in Edinburgh so had company for the last part of the tedious trail. We managed to raise transport eventually from Crail station and checked into HMS *Jackdaw* well into the evening. The air station, situated north of Crail on the eastern tip of Fife was buzzing with life. Reception was in the Officers block between the mess and the wardroom. The former had been cleared for dancing. The latter was full to overflowing with people. Being fatigued from our journey, Alan and I decided to find our cabins and turn in. The accommodation was individual and very well appointed. Washed and refreshed we decided to return to the wardroom and investigate.

As we entered, we met officers we had last seen as ratings on our course at Gosport. They had undergone flying training in UK and had thus got ahead of us during our passage to and from Canada. Perched on a table twixt mess and wardroom they were bored. They complained about the absence of the fair sex. I entered the wardroom and stood just inside the doorway to observe. At once a Wren steward approached with a tray bearing drinks and offered me one. I'd but sipped it when a tipsy Lieutenant with a girl on his arm approached me. "Would you be kind enough to look after this young lady?" he requested and straightway tottered off. Naturally, I endeavoured to please, it being apparently my first duty at my new station. So it was that within two minutes of entering the building I crossed from wardroom to dance hall in front of my bored and disappointed colleagues with a young lady on my arm. They were astounded, so was I, come to that. Never again did I experience such a welcoming at a naval air station. I know not what the party was about, but the drinks and buffet refreshments were on the house.

This incident led to an enjoyable diversion during some of my off duty hours. I much liked meeting people, but disliked being one of a crowd — preferred quiet company rather than carousals. Anyway, the young lady I escorted proved to be the schoolteacher daughter of the Warrant Officer Paymaster, home on leave for Christmas. The lass apparently did not dislike her dancing partner, though my prowess on the dance floor was a shade dodgy. No doubt our alcoholic libations enabled both of us to overcome our lack of practice and worked as a catalyst. Hence I was invited to the home some evenings during the holiday for company, entertainment and an introduction to the game *Mah-jong*, a rather complicated calculating activity the rules of which I have sadly forgotten. One did not normally see eye to eye with paymasters, but there you are. I felt that I was developing a sense of belonging to a wider Navy in which there were many necessary specialities as well as flying.

Having been spoiled by my reception, I was soon to experience the other side of the coin. On 29th December we met up with our instructors in ramshackle huts reminiscent of those thrown together by allotment tenants. Facilities were nil. Although there was lying snow and mud, I was soon up for my first familiarisation flight round the training area in an Albacore. This was the real thing. I was with pilots who had been 'on the job'.

The introduction to the aircraft we were to fly was a historic occasion. After experiencing Tiger Moths and Harvards, it was like transferring from a Mini to a heavy service vehicle. Both of the naval TBR(Torpedo bomber reconnaissance) biplanes, the Albacore and Swordfish, stood over twelve feet high. Boarding them

The Fairey Albacore.

was quite a problem, struggling with handholds, footholds and a parachute. If one started with the wrong foot on the wheel of an Albacore, it was impossible to get into the cockpit. The only recourse was to return to earth and start again. Things were made difficult because, for protective reasons, the aircraft were widely dispersed. This necessitated a trek across sloplly terrain in flying boots to find and identify them, scrape the snow and frost off and then start them.

The Albacore had an enclosed cockpit with perspex protection and the pilot had a forward view unencumbered by the wings. In my experience, the view became dimmed by oil which spread from its radial engine to the screen, which never seemed to be clear. The aircraft, although having smooth lines for a biplane, was heavy to handle and unresponsive.

The Swordfish, which looked singularly Heath Robinson, somehow had more appeal for me. True it was cold, very cold in winter snow, with an open cockpit, forward visibility was poor, petrol and oil tanks fronted by a radial engine were sited directly in front of the pilot whose cockpit was abaft the wings. This was the age of the Spitfire, smooth, speedy, sophisticated. I should have felt dismayed on seeing the aircraft I was to fly. It was not conceived from the craft competing for the Schneider Trophy, but was more like a camel — a horse designed by a committee. It was metal framed and fabric covered, anointed liberally with dope, a plethora of struts and wires, a fixed undercarriage, no flaps, a metal three bladed fixed pitch propeller. It could attain a speed of one hundred and ten knots at best, from its Bristol Pegasus engine. It was first produced by Fairey Aviation in 1935. It was the maid of all work in the Fleet Air Arm — still the same six years on. As I say, I should have felt dismayed, disillusioned and disappointed but somehow I wasn't. It was the Swordfish that I was to fly as a TBR pilot, so I had better learn to fly it. 'Stringbag' it might well be described with every justification from its appearance, but, with able pilots, it had done sterling work by the time I was introduced to it. In two months, with guidance from seasoned pilots, I had to understand the aircraft's handling techniques, its limitations and its strike potential.

One feature probably peculiar to the Swordfish was the antiquated method of starting it up. A mechanic stood on the lower mainplane taking care not to interfere with the locking bolt, which secured the wing in the 'spread' position and hand cranked the inertia wheel — very like a barrel organ, but requiring infinitely more effort. Petrol on and wheel humming, the pilot engaged the engine and hoped it would fire. If it didn't, one started again. In inclement conditions it was a burdensome task for the 'cranker', a firm foothold being difficult at times.

Exercises were performed in both types of aircraft — general flying, formation, torpedo carrying, landing with torpedo and attack procedures. Simulated torpedo attacks from altitude required 10,000 feet plus. It took a considerable time to reach the desired height in a Swordfish. Descending was different. To my surprise, I found that the craft could be thrown about, tight turns could be executed and evasive action taken that gave one confidence. Delivering a torpedo was different. One had to be straight and level, at the correct height, not exceeding 120 knots, have the skill to determine the speed and direction of the target by observation of the sea conditions, the bow wave of the vessel and its size. The angle by which one offset the drop from ones approach line to the target was determined by reference to the sight — a bar extending each side of and ahead of the pilots screen. The bar was surmounted by a number of beads. The spacing between the beads represented the adjustment to be made for target speed and range so that the torpedo would be on a closing course with the target.

One could appreciate the virtues and perceive the shortcomings of the Swordfish. Being underpowered, it took aeons to achieve a commanding height. Manoeuvrability when losing height was splendid. Reduced speed and level flight at the torpedo dropping stage, which was at fairly close range, was critical, so ability to depart from the scene at speed could not be achieved. Quite problematical was a torpedo attack on a moving target! The Swordfish was not equipped to launch a torpedo from a low level approach. It would have difficulty in avoiding attack whilst getting within range. We practised attacks, formation flying and other exercises in cold snowy weather and became acclimatised to open cockpits and numb fingers.

During the first week of our course, there was a fatality. Two aircraft flown by members of the overlapping earlier course collided in the air. One of the pilots was on his own ground. He lived in Crail. It was a shock, especially as I had met him.

I had another setback. The Captain of the station determined that flying personnel were unfit. He therefore decreed that we attend the gym early in the mornings for a work out. Unfortunately, in my performing a vault over a large horse, end on, a mistake was made by the PO physical instructor who failed to support me, causing me to fall heavily and breaking my nose. Reporting to the MO did not help. He merely suggested that I should leave it until the following day when the bleeding should have abated. Reporting the following day resulted in no treatment being given and criticism made to the effect that I should have reported the accident earlier. My protestations fell on deaf ears. Very much Catch 22. I continued flying without any lay off. The effect of sudden changes in pressure through climbing and diving not surprisingly had a deleterious effect. The injury gave me trouble throughout my service although some treatment was attempted on occasions. It ultimately resulted in a comprehensive and unpleasant operation sixteen years later, by which time I could only breathe with difficulty.

Another happening disturbed me greatly. The local people were hospitable and, being in Scotland, there was Hogmany. I recall setting out through a foot of standing snow with a colleague who knew the ropes. The procedure was to take a bottle and 'gang' in and out of the dwellings in Crail getting progressively more friendly and more inebriated. We also attended a dance a consequence of which was that my friends Alan and Bobby Campbell were invited to the home of a retired brigadier by his two daughters the following week for a social evening. Tragedy followed. I sat alongside Bobby at breakfast one day before the visit was due. He was an architectural student from Liverpool, a warm hearted charming lad beloved by us all. At lunchtime he was absent — gone for ever. In practising evasive action in a Swordfish, flying low over the sea he misjudged things, dipped a wingtip into the water and was killed. It was the first time that a death had meant so much to me. I felt personally involved and very emotionally charged. The world seemed a cruel place.

Alan telephoned the young ladies he and Bobby were due to visit and told them of Bobby's death. The response he received was callous in the extreme. There was no expression of sorrow or sympathy. Instead the suggestion made was "Well, bring somebody else". My sorrow was compounded with anger.

I completed the course unscathed, apart of course from the proboscis, and was well pleased to manage an above average marking from the CO who was one of the heroes of the Taranto raid. My two months with 786 Squadron at HMS *Jackdaw* was most valuable experience.

Just one more river to cross to complete my operational training, just four more concentrated weeks. We moved north to HMS *Condor* at Arbroath. That sounded as though we were going up a bit after *Jackdaw*. We were to fly Albacores and Swordfish, predominantly the latter. The course concentrated on deck landing instruction, instrument flying, night flying, formation night flying and depth charge dropping. Once we had mastered these, we would be capable of using all the offensive weaponry carried by the aircraft and controlled by the pilot — torpedoes, bombs, depth charges and forward firing gun.

The snow moderated so that underfoot it was better than at Crail. One could taxi an aircraft more easily after starting up without the danger of depositing the craft on its nose, because the wheels were embedded in mud. It was easily done if one advanced the throttle incautiously.

One night I had my fill of familiarisation with flying in the dark. I was up for four hours, first doing a short spell of night formation then a long one of course steering. Flying up and down over the North Sea in a Swordfish on a cold black night, taking care not to lose sight of a signal light and the dim illumination of the airfield was wearing. I was fearful of getting lost.

One flew a Swordfish all the time. The aircraft could not be trimmed so that it would maintain a straight and level course. If you were airborne for four hours you were very much 'hands on' for two hundred and forty minutes. Various adjustments were made by pilots in consultation with their riggers, to their own aircraft to effect something like stability using parachute elastic, sticking bits on the rudder and so on, but they could not be flown 'hands off' even if stability was improved.

Deck landing practise was a new experience. There was, of course, no deck, so a simulated deck was marked out on a runway and we had to learn to do a three point landing at a specific point. The landing speed and the angle of approach was critical. Guidance was given by the 'batsman' by signalling to the pilot with two paddles or bats. Pre-arranged signals indicated the corrections in speed, angle, line of approach etc which he considered necessary. The landing circuit height was much lower than that with which RAF pilots would be familiar and the approach speeds much lower. Whereas RAF aircraft would touch down and run a considerable distance before coming to a standstill, naval aircraft had to touch down and stop. It was essential that when the aircraft was just above the point of touchdown in a three point attitude(the way it would stand on the ground) the throttle was closed and the stick pulled back, that it lost flying speed and dropped. Too fast an approach, even marginally so and, on the stick being pulled back, the aircraft would float on instead of grounding. Having got the idea, we had to do the landings with the arrester hook down so as to engage with the wires set out in the landing area. Being jerked to a halt was initially quite alarming.

We did more formation flying, instrument flying and depth charge dropping then we were through. I achieved a good report on my deck landing efforts, did satisfactory with the other specialities and was adjudged OK.

I had completed my formal training, which had taken twelve months. What would happen next. I had my fingers crossed.

Chapter 5 — Fledged but Frustrated

After a short leave, I received orders to report to 833 Squadron at HMS *Landrail*, Machrihanish, a first line squadron. I was delighted to have made it. That was a long journey from Manchester — train to Glasgow then by MacBraynes aged bus on a scenic but uncomfortable ride by Dumbarton, Tarbet, Inverary, Tarbert, the West coast of the Mull of Kintyre, down by Kilbracken Sound to Campbeltown, thence by station transport to Machrihanish. At least I enjoyed seeing Loch Lomond, Loch Fyne and Loch Tarbert.

Delight turned to dismay on discovering that Lieutenant Housser, a Canadian who joined our course in Kingston as an officer, and I, both drafted to 833, were supernumerary. The squadron had a full complement, was 'worked up' and ready for operations. The Commanding Officer, Lieutenant Stephens RN, a direct hard swearing character kept me with the squadron for his own convenience against the time for embarkation leave which was almost due. "Kept me in the squadron" was a minimal spell. I did only one weeks flying, but in that week packed in some valuable experience of what was expected. Curiously it included my flying Housser to Prestwick after a couple of days because he had managed to wangle both an extension of his leave and also a lift to the most convenient railway service. Feeling the comradeship of a squadron was new and rewarding for, although I was a sprog and not remaining with 833, I was made to feel welcome. The drive and support of the CO impressed me. I was sorry not to be on the strength.

On my arrival I met squadron member Frank Cowtan whom I had seen before during training. He was due to fly the night I reported for duty, but found that he was down for duty as Air Watch Officer. He asked if I would stand in for him and I agreed. At the relieving hour I crossed to the far side of the airfield and made myself known to the officer on duty. He handed me the orders pertaining to the AWO's duties, a tome the size of a bumper telephone directory and made himself scarce. I set to make myself familiar with my duties and ploughed into the instructions. I'd covered the first half dozen pages when I found that I had company. Company in the form of a Commander who seemed to be out of sorts. Perhaps that understates his condition. He was puce. True, it was dusk and I could therefore not be categorical on the point, but that is how he appeared.

He roared a question. "Why are the lights not on at Ugadale?" Never having heard of Ugadale I could make no satisfactory reply and confessed that I had no idea. A staccato series of equally incomprehensible questions were fired at me. I failed on them all. It appeared probable that my career as a naval officer, acting, temporary, probationary was coming to an abrupt end when something I stuttered revealed that I had not yet been on the station for twenty four hours. On learning this, he diverted from my misdeeds and heaped strongly adverse criticism at the powers that had permitted me to pose as an AWO. I was grudgingly excused. I had learned a lesson on naval responsibility. Except in dire emergency, do not undertake tasks for which you are singularly ill equipped. It was a different reception from Crail!

My friend Frank got away without much trouble probably because, being involved in night flying practise he wasn't readily available and later the Commander's temper had abated. His only worry was when I was allotted his aircraft to fly. His anxiety was such that he clambered aboard. I somewhat resented his questioning my prowess. Later I appreciated how much a pilot was attached to his plane, the plane over which he had spent considerable time perfecting its performance by discussion with his fitter and rigger and making trial and error adjustments.

An incident occurred one night when the squadron undertook an exercise attacking a towed target which represented a submarine. One pilot and his observer found the attack quite realistic because the towing vessels crew, local seamen, being nervous and trigger fingered, fired a fusillade of tracer bullets at the aircraft. Fortunately none found their mark and the pilot in relating the experience had the conviction that it was as he put it 'pretend stuff'. He could not bring himself to accept that it was 'for real'. Such things did not happen in the Clyde. Or could they? Much later I experienced vessels in the convoy we were escorting, or rather their crews, firing upon our aircraft whilst they were on a landing circuit.

Appointment to a first line squadron entitled one by custom to something the new member prized — an Irvine jacket — that leather fur lined garment which would replace or complement the gabardine Sidcot used throughout our training. Shortly after my arrival with 833, disregarding my anticipated brief stay there, I sought out the stores, presented myself and requested of the Stores Petty Officer that I be furnished with my prize. He was reluctant to supply me and justified his reluctance to do so by posing questions. "Are you proceeding to Northern waters beyond the Arctic Circle" was one such. I replied that it was not given to me to know where the squadron was going. Other squadron members had Irvine jackets. I wanted one. He became quite stuffy and, refusing to hand over, sent me off with a flea in my ear.

Returning to the squadron office feeling very disappointed and no doubt appearing downcast, I was spotted by the CO who was just emerging from the building. He instantly observed my demeanour and demanded "What the hell's wrong with you?" I told him of my interview with the Stores PO. He turned on his heel, strode back into the office, seized the telephone and asked for the stores. His stentorian tones over the wires in forthright and unambiguous language caused me to wonder why he used the phone at all. He could have been heard clearly on a stormy day on a decent sized parade ground. His peroration was brief. He slammed the instrument back on to its pad, turned and addressed me. "Go," he said, pointing imperiously in the direction of the stores department, "and get one and make sure it's a damned good one".

I scuttled off to find the stores PO a changed man. He was most obsequious, almost had the manner of a Moss Brothers senior salesman at his most attentive. On his knees he was as he beseeched me to select just what I wanted from his stock. I emerged resplendent. Joseph in his multi coloured dreamcoat could not have out done me. It was with regret that I accepted that I would not be serving under this most supportive Commanding Officer.

On 29th April, 833 Squadron went on embarkation leave and I went on 'who knows where' leave. The officers were a lively, inventive, enthusiastic crew and none more so than one of the observers, 'Flossie' Howells. He either took on or was directed by the CO to make any necessary arrangements for our departure from HMS *Landrail*. He did so in a somewhat unorthodox manner.

His reasoning was thus. If leave commenced on 29th April, it commenced at 0001 on 29th April. This reasoning was diametrically opposed to that of the Station Commander, to whom you have already been introduced. His understanding of departing on leave was a parade and inspection after breakfast which would result in wasting much of the day travelling. The road journey from Machrihanish to Glasgow was long and tedious. Howell's arrangements were most careful, calculated and clandestine. A number of the officers had assignations in London on 29th and were desirous of being on the early morning train from Glasgow. Speed was of the essence.

Shortly before midnight on the 28th a fleet of Macbraynes elderly coaches trundled into the station. All squadron members were ready to board without delay. So far as the wardroom party was concerned I can remember there were boisterous high spirits, after all we'd been in the wardroom all evening. I also recall that a crate of beer was stowed in our coach, the driver was clearly advised that he was to make no stop other than at the 'Rest and be Thankful' and that most briefly for the convenience of the passengers, that he was confidently expected to reduce the normal journey time by one hour (this at night) and that there was some consideration forthcoming if he was at the station in time for us to be able to catch the train.

At 0001 29th April the convoy of coaches was away. Whether or not the Commander was apprised of the scheme I don't know but, arrangements having been closed with Macbraynes, he was not able to countermand them. The driver met the time schedule. The journey was a bit hairy and could have been unnerving but, probably due to the anaesthetic effect of our ale, we hardly noticed.

I left 833 Squadron somewhat regretfully for ever and Machrihanish for the first of many times. My short experience with the squadron had been exciting and valuable. My mind turned over what might befall me next.

Chapter 6 — Fully Fledged

Following my unexpected bonus leave, I was ordered to report to HMS *Daedalus*, Lee on the Solent there to join 835 Squadron. Daedalus was the Fleet Air Arm HQ, the most prestigious of the naval air stations with splendid accommodation and facilities. Unlike many other stations it was not situated miles from civilisation on some weather beaten outpost.

835 Squadron had existed for a few months in a miniature form having but four aircraft, four pilots and four observers. The introduction for the 'old timers' was on

the *Andalucia Star* a luxury appointed vessel of the Blue Star Line, in which they cruised in consummate ease to Kingston, Jamaica. Shipboard romances it seems, were commonplace because, also taking passage were several ladies — officers wives and others. These were terminated just in time, due to the speed of the vessel. The aircraft were taken up and flown up the eastern seaboard of the United States to Norfolk, Virginia. Return to the UK was made on HMS *Furious* from which a small amount of patrol flying took place.

I was one of four pilots additional to the existing members sent to bring the squadron up to something like strength. The others were Lieutenant Harry 'Hank' Housser, RCNVR, to whom I felt I was attached but not in an endearing way — more like being followed in one's car at an unsafe distance by a heavy goods vehicle. He was large, domineering and self opinionated. The other pilot Sub Lieutenants were Bob Selley and Jim Urquart, a Devonian and a Scot. There were also two observers, Sub Lieutenant John Winstanley and Midshipman Dave Newberry. Of the original eight, seven remained —pilots Gwyn Jones 'Taffy', Robin Shirley-Smith, Johnny Hunt; observers Ted Barringer, Jack Teesdale, Stan Thomas and Jack Parker all of whom were Sub Lieutenants. The original Commanding Officer, Johnny Johnson, went elsewhere and a new CO was appointed. He was John Lang, Lieutenant RN.

Things were new and strange. We had to get to know each other. *Daedalus* had a slightly melancholy air. The delayed shock still persisted from the tragic loss of lives and aircraft by 825 Squadron only three months before in its courageous but futile attack on the German battlecruisers *Scharnhorst* and *Gneisenau* as they slipped through the English Channel. Only five aircrew survived. Swordfish aircraft were ill equipped to deliver a torpedo attack in such inclement weather, negligible visibility and without any fighter escort. I think that 825 Squadron was in course of being reformed about the time we were crewing up.

We gradually settled down, were paired off into crews and allocated aircraft. I found myself with Winstanley, 'Winnie', an observer of short stature, rather comical appearance and disconcerting differently coloured eyes. He could be quite amusing in a flippant way but, I felt, not so concentrated and down to earth when it mattered. We got on quite reasonably, introduced ourselves to our aircraft, a new Swordfish powered with a Pegasus 30 engine, number DK684H and our ground crew. Our rigger McLean, was a really handsome fellow whose appearance, he stood well over six feet, reminded me of the imposing seaman on the old Players cigarette packets. He bore a distinguished nautical air proper to the Senior Service, yet was of most gentle demeanour.

The Commanding Officer, John Lang, was an observer. To me it seemed wrong, because I had expectations of a pilot CO, one who would have experienced the problems I had to face and could give advice and guidance. However he was the CO, the Senior Officer, an RN Lieutenant with operational experience of flying off the Norwegian coast, the Atlantic and the Mediterranean. I found myself respecting the

Commanding Officer and his senior rank than respecting the man. He was neither supportive nor inspiring, but rather diffident and regrettably humourless. The senior pilot, by rank, was Lieutenant Housser. He being on my training course, had no more experience than I — virtually none. The 'old timer' pilots in the squadron had precious little, they had just been in longer. It was obvious to be a good pilot I had to learn for myself.

One feature of *Daedalus*, different from other naval air stations was that it possessed a Gunroom as well as a Wardroom. Only officers of the rank of lieutenant and above were vouchsafed the dignity and quieter atmosphere of the Wardroom. It followed that Lang and Housser gravitated there in off duty evening hours. So their socialising with the rest of the squadron officers was minimal. One normally had to serve satisfactorily as a sub lieutenant for two and a half years before being promoted to lieutenant. A curious anomaly was that a sub lieutenant over twenty five years of age could, under the same conditions, be promoted after six months. After my brief of 833 Squadron, I found the comparison disappointing, but I was grateful to be in a first line squadron and anxious to become proficient and get into action.

835 Squadron was at Lee on Solent but one month before moving to the Orkney's. In that month I managed to benefit from many new experiences and become familiar and comfortable with the aircraft.

An early job that fell to me was to pilot my plane with the squadron photographer aboard. He was to make a vertical plot of Lee and Fleetlands. The Swordfish had to be flown. It could not be trimmed to fly straight and level. This must seem odd to present day pilots who traverse the globe sitting relaxed, observing the instruments and enjoying an after dinner coffee. Once strapped into a cockpit in the Swordfish with not overmuch room, it was not possible to move around. Creature comforts were non existent and it was desirable, most desirable, to visit the heads before any flight. This presented no problem at Lee in the warm early summer of 1942, but it was to become most troublesome on some later colder occasions.

Discussions with the rigger, resulting in trial and error adjustments to the trim by Heath Robinson methods, could be made to improve things somewhat, but grid photography was exacting. Flying a dead level course at dead level height, steady speed, making precision even turns on to an exactly reciprocal course, observing what was going on outside the aircraft whilst the photographer took his shots on a huge biscuit tin of a camera over the side of the aircraft, was concentrated stuff. Once the film had been developed, printed and the grid assembled, evidence of the pilots accuracy was clear for all to see. Fortunately, my efforts were up to scratch and the end result regarded as satisfactory. It was an interesting and instructive task demonstrating the importance of accurate instrument flying.

Normally one got airborne by lining up on the runway, advancing the throttle, surging forward, or trundling forward in the case of the Swordfish, gaining airspeed and effecting lift off by gentle backward pressure on the control column. There were other methods. One was to use a catapult.

The one on which we were to practice was sighted nearby on a grass landing ground at Gosport. Whether or not we'd ever use one on operations we were not to know, but the drill had to be learned. In mid May I flew to Gosport with Lieutenant Housser as passenger. The aircraft was secured to the catapult contraption, my passenger having disembarked, and instructions were given by the control officer. Strict observation of the signals made by the holding up of red and or blue flags or both struck was essential. Once the catapult had been loaded and the appropriate signal given, the pilot prepared to go. The throttle was advanced 'through the gate' to full power and the thumb screw tightened so that it would not slip back. Above the pilot's head by the top mainplane — quite a reach from the cockpit — was a knurled knob about four inches in diameter. This had to be rotated anticlockwise so as to depress the narrow slats on the top wing. The seven degree angle resulting gave the correct additional lift to assist in getting airborne from the catapult. The 'take off' flag was dropped. All being prepared and one waited with expectancy. It was strange and unpredictable, because the precise take off moment could not be judged.

It was not "On your marks, get set, go". Rather was it "Ready, now I'm going to fool you". "When's it going to fire? How long? — Look out we're off!".

Reflexes were now tested. The aircraft shot forward. Full power was essential. The thumb screw worked loose. The throttle lever slipped back. Power was reduced. My left hand shoved it forward to maintain power. The right hand held the stick, as always, to keep the plane straight and level. Feet controlled the rudder. There was one other dimension. The slats lowered for take off gave lift but, once airborne, caused drag so that the aforementioned knurled knob had to be rotated clockwise at once if one was to remain airborne and fly away. Pilots in general have two arms and a pair of hands. For the thirty seconds after a catapult launch the Swordfish pilot needed three. Any observer witnessing his contortions might well assume it to be a form of lightning semaphore.

I got away OK, returned, was loaded on the catapult and did it again. Then I did it with Housser as passenger before flying him back to Lee. A fortnight later I did it another couple of times taking up a member of the ground crew for a 'flip'. I made my mark on the frame of the catapult. If one took off and flew majestically away with out mishap one signed on one side of the catapult. That I did. If, instead, one misjudged things and hit the ground on take off one signed on the other side. The signatures were about evenly divided.

Dummy torpedo drops and bombing practice helped to perfect our pilot skills. We also had to get used to knitting into effective teams with our observers. Up to date, our flying had been solo. Now and for ever in our TBR squadron things were to be different. We were responsible now, not just for ourselves and the aircraft, but for our crew.

One routine, which had to be performed efficiently, was wind finding. We were to discover much later, when flying operational in the Atlantic, that on occasions it was decreed that we maintain radio silence and fly by dead reckoning navigation.

Flying to and from a moving base using this method concentrated the mind marvellously. It was quite different from every man's experience driving the family car relying on his spouse as a navigator. One could not stop, look at the map, or enquire of some passer by for directions.

Weather information on shipboard was as accurate as the Met Officers could provide. They did a splendid job, but weather conditions at sea change considerably in quite short periods. It was therefore essential that to navigate with certainty one was dependent upon the wind strengths and directions used being as near as correct as possible. Windfinding was a combined operation. Flying on a steady course and altitude, a smoke float was dropped into the sea. The course was maintained for a stipulated brief time determined by the observer, a steady even turn was made on to the reciprocal course, the new course maintained for the same time as before and an exactly similar 180 degree turn made onto the original course. The observer took beam and quarter bearings on the smoke float as the plane reached the appropriate positions and from the figures recorded he calculated the wind strength and direction. At a comfortable desk it would have been a deal easier than it was with an unsecured board in an open cockpit. At night it was even more difficult for the observer with minimum lighting in the cockpit and imperfect vision of the flame float used, which behaved like a flashing or occulting light as it bobbed up and down in the waves. In some of the conditions experienced, it wasn't any easier for the pilot either. No night flying was done by the squadron at Lee. The nocturnal adventures were to be enjoyed later.

I have mentioned the cohesion of the team of pilot and observer. The full crew was to be three, pilot, observer and rear gunner but like the trireme, if I may liken the Swordfish to that ancient galley, not with three sets of oars, but with three tiers of shared responsibility. It was not fully established at Lee. It was at HMS *Sparrowhawk*, Hatston in Orkney that we got fully organised.

At home, before joining the Navy, I used my cycle a great deal. I found it more convenient, more reliable and speedier than our local public transport. Squadron offices were distant from the Officers block at Lee and I considered that my cycle might be useful. I therefore arranged by some means to get my lightweight fixed wheel cycle, a Raleigh, to Lee and on the strength. Transporting it from thence by air attracted comment. A wheel strapped to the supporting struts on each side twixt the wings gave a balanced effect and the false impression to some that the Swordfish had some mysterious secret equipment. The frame was less obvious, being strapped beneath the belly.

On 10th June 1942 I was on the air party and flew carrying a PO maintenance mechanic, my cycle and high hopes via Catterick, Crail thence to Hatston which was close to Kirkwall on the Orkney mainland.

The squadron moves, of which 835 had many, were much more comfortable for the pilots flying the planes and carrying the necessary complement of ground crew members for maintenance purposes than for the rest of the squadron. Loading stores and equipment, packing and unpacking and arranging transportation was heavy work, time consuming and disruptive. I was fortunate to find myself flying pretty well every time we moved. The only concern was that one's own personal gear was cared for. There was no boot in a Swordfish! One had to trust to luck. On occasions something or other went adrift. On this first occasion I was delighted to have the easier passage over a seven hundred and fifty plus miles move — our longest.

Chapter 7 — Orkney Interlude

The flight was pleasant and uneventful. A new experience was that of flying in formation over such a distance. It was early summer. The days were long — even longer as we flew North to HMS *Sparrowhawk*, Hatston. The airfield with lush green grass had runways but ninety feet wide, different from most air stations. This width approximated to the width of the deck of a fleet carrier. We did a stream landing aiming to get all six aircraft down in minimum time. This was a regular routine for naval aircraft. At sea a carrier had to be committed to a steady course directly into the wind to receive aircraft and during the period the course was maintained it was vulnerable to enemy attack. Hence, if several aircraft were to land at the same time they did so at very short intervals. As 'tail end Charlie' of the formation, which had formed into echelon I found myself with no runway on which to land because the fifth pilot had not backed up smartly enough on number four, once down, to give me landing room. Consequently I found myself putting down on the perimeter track in front of the hangars and performing an unscheduled adjustment to my course as I negotiated the chicane made up of a barbed wire security fence which part obstructed my landing path. It was an anxious moment but I did not intend to distinguish myself by going round the circuit again. As it happened, number five did ease my problem by running off the tarmac on to the grass and affording me some stopping space. It took only minutes after we had taxied off the runway and parked, before Number Five was summoned to present himself at the Air Watch Office and required to explain why he ran onto the grass. The green sward was precious to the Lieutenant Commander Flying (Wings) as we quickly discovered. It looked like bowling green turf. He was not interested in the strength or direction of the winds which were a predominant feature of the Orkney. Cross wind landings were commonplace.

Considering that the station was something of an outpost, it was quite well appointed. The wardroom had one unusual feature — the best stocked bar I experienced in the whole of my service. How that came about I don't know. The Officer being designated to the task of stocking up had obviously excelled himself, even to the extent of obtaining exotic liqueurs, "alcoholic beverages flavoured to be more agreeable to the taste" as the dictionary has it, which we had never heard of. When we arrived we found there had been a decree that bar stocks should be reduced to something like normal. This resulted in many squadron members doing their level best to assist in that direction subject to the exigencies of their mess bill limits which, with reduced prices obtaining, were not stringent.

In keeping with the luxurious standard of after dinner living, the Station Commander insisted that Officers wear bow ties to dinner.

We had not been obliged to do that at *Daedalus*, the HQ, but the Commander was 'boss cat' and that was that. The one and only gents outfitter at Kirkwall profited from the rule and did not give bow ties away.

Once the full squadron had assembled and got sorted out, we set to with a work up programme so that we'd be prepared for action. This included depth charge dropping, low level and dive bombing, torpedo attacks, firing practice for our Telegraphist Air Gunner with his gas operated .303 machine gun and ADDLS, Aerodrome dummy deck landings — against the time we found an aircraft carrier. There was a standby against the possibility of the *Admiral Hipper* putting to sea from Norwegian waters. I recall being kitted up in the Air Watch Office and reading without artificial light until 2.0am on one occasion. No enemy presence was reported. There was no real action. One unusual item I note from my flying log — "Air to air firing — front gun" — like the air gunners, a Browning .303. This was a rare one for the Swordfish.

One exhilarating and instructive attack was against the capital ships in Scapa Flow. We climbed to something above ten thousand feet, which took ages in a loaded Swordfish and dived to torpedo the *King George V*. There were some Albacores and RAF Beauforts with us in the dummy attack. The manoeuvrability of the Swordfish descending was outstanding. One could do tight turns, vary speeds and really throw the robust aircraft about. Defending the target were RAF Spitfires. Regrettably one of these and the pilot was lost in the sea whilst trying to keep beads on a Swordfish down to the water. We were delighted with the performance of our planes and were getting confident of our fighter evasion tactics when we met our Waterloo — a squadron of Gloster Gladiators. We couldn't elude them. If our manoeuvrability was outstanding, their's was superb. I longed from that moment to fly a Gladiator but never got the chance.

Work up procedures were essential, but could become tedious. It followed that like other pilots I indulged in some unofficial and unapproved flying. This was a good thing because it gave one confidence and a bit of initiative. One learned what the aircraft would and would not do. Low flying was part of our routine but how low could I fly? The sea was for once like a mill pond. Could I bounce my wheels on the water? It required very accurate flying. Only a little too low and I'd upend the plane into the briny. I tried and did it quite nicely. Mind you, I nearly lost the observer, because he was not wearing his 'G String', his safety harness and consequently nearly left the aircraft without warning. A thing to remember when flying low over land or sea was the aerial which was trailed by the TAG from the rear cockpit. It was extended in varying lengths to tune his crystal controlled transmitter receiver. Many must have been lost because they were not reeled in before any unscheduled escapades. A lost aerial required an explanation. Being out of radio communication was also wrong.

Executing a loop in a Swordfish was uncommon, but not impossible. There was, of course, the danger of losing something. Nipping 'twixt the Old Man of Hoy and the mainland was forbidden, but feasible. Orkney had glorious silvery beaches seemingly remote form human presence. Seals sunned themselves by the shore and often we deliberately disturbed their siestas. These extra mural activities did not appear in our log books.

I found my cycle innovation to be most useful at Hatston, but also tiresome. My cycle being the only one, other officers borrowed it without leave or request. Because of this I made a cardboard indicator and hung it on the Squadron Office wall. A pointer showed who had borrowed my steed and whence he had gone. It was useless. Either it was not operated or the borrower took the bike away and neglected to return it. That left me to search for it and it certainly got around the station. I fancy that I made the most use of it — marginally.

Another innovation was quickly taken up. A jacket with brass buttons and gold lace was, in very little time, reduced to something like a garment acquired from a charity shop. Wearing flying gear topped by a parachute harness ruined clothes. I discovered that we could be permitted to wear a navy blue battledress suit and at once got in touch with Paisley's, the naval outfitters in Glasgow. They made one to measure for me. In no time most of the squadron had them. The Commander did not rule that we had to don bow ties with them, but they were out of order for dinner.

Sport occupied most of my off duty hours. I had been brought up to soccer and played for the squadron team. One disadvantage was that the pitches were on open exposed ground and the wind blew almost incessantly when we played. When the ball went out of play it took much time and exertion to recover it. The wettest place we ever played was the Isle of Flotta in the south of Scapa Flow to which delectable venue we were transported through driving rain on the deck of a drifter. The pitch was so wet that it was almost impossible to keep one's footing let alone kick a ball.

Hockey was a new game to me and I enjoyed it. It was faster than I had anticipated and, though I reckoned to be fleet of foot, I found myself, under directions from the Senior officer, to be expected to cover the pitch at the rate of a gazelle. It seemed to me that on most stations where hockey was played, either the Captain or Commander captained the team from centre half or centre forward and all bellowed orders regarding my positioning. There was no loitering for Sadler at outside right in a naval hockey team.

I did not care to be one of a crowd therefore, though not abstemious, the size of my mess bills were academic. Reading, writing, sketching and absorbing poetry I found rewarding. 'Hitting the bottle' was a meaningless waste of time as were riotous assemblies. Getting out with a colleague was good, as was female company on the dance floor, cinema or walking out. There was need to be cautious about the last relationships. It was only with some delicacy and tact that these remained platonic friendships. The Orkney Wrens were not backward in coming forward.

One evening after dinner I was perched at the bar with Robin Shirley–Smith. He and I got on quite well. Of course, as with all relationships, we had things in common and things over which we disagreed. The former far exceeded the latter.

Robin was a little above the average age of 835 Squadron members, a trainee architect, interrupted from his studies by the inconvenience of war and rather serious minded. A big fellow, hirsute everywhere except his cranium, but clean shaven, he adopted an air of seniority the which was in keeping with his appearance. He could be likened to the character 'Winchester' in MASH. If matters of moment were to be discussed, or important visitors arrived, 'Shirley' needed no encouragement to step forward and assume the role of Senior member. Anyway, Shirley and I were having a civilised chat over a glass and a smoke oblivious to the raucous activities going on at the far end of the Wardroom. It was sufficiently long to afford the two of us, the only ones at the bar, the licence to dissociate ourselves form the discordant din.

Into the bar came an American Air Force Officer seeking refreshment. We looked at the visitor and instantly recognised him. It was Douglas Fairbanks.

My readiness to dispense hospitality was swept aside by Shirley. Normally he was a mite slow in that department, but not on this occasion. In a trice he was in charge. He ordered drinks and joined conversation. Naturally he had to overdo things. He could not forego this heavensent opportunity to display his knowledge and experience. I could hardly get a word in, nor could Douglas Fairbanks come to that. It was such a shame that he went too far, because he was coming over in fine authoritative style.

Fairbanks, a perfect gentleman, and a highly intelligent person, listened politely although no doubt chagrined by the attitude Shirley adopted. It was much on the lines of Shirley's experiences. One would never have guessed that before his wartime enlistment he was a trainee architect. The impression given was that he had vouchsafed to the Wright Brothers a few wrinkles as to how to set about getting airborne. As I say, he overdid it. His overblown oration simply had to be interrupted. It was, in a most gentle and polite manner.

Taking a golden opportunity when Shirley, of necessity, paused for breath, Fairbanks enquired with quite a deferential air "Tell me, were you flying in the First War?" It was the first and, I think, the only occasion when Shirley was lost for words. I even enjoyed the opportunity of having a word or two with Douglas Fairbanks before he left to fly off from his Orkney interlude.

During the period of our working up exercises and the gaining of familiarity with the aircraft I experienced some reversals. These confirmed my conviction that life was not fair. Of course I had reached that conclusion whilst still a schoolboy. Confronted with uncomprehending and insurmountable senior authority in the Senior Service, I felt at times frustrated and almost rebellious.

The first incident was in June '42. The squadron was airborne on exercise. We were in loose formation out to the North East of Orkney when I noticed that the engine temperature gauge registered too high a reading. Something was amiss, be it the instrument or the engine. I determined that emergency action was necessary. Confirmation with Winstanley, my observer, that the airfield at Twatt in Orkney was the nearest land resolved matters. I broke formation, headed there and landed without mishap. I had, as I saw it, logically reasoned that its being but an exercise 'twas better to be safe than sorry. Terra firma was my goal not the North Sea, which would risk the lives of my observer, rear gunner as well as myself and write off of an aircraft.

Inspection of the Swordfish revealed no faults. After a short time the temperature gauge registered normal and, finding no obstacle to our returning to Hatston I flew back cautiously eyes glued on the instrument which remained steady, without further alarms.

On my reporting at the Squadron Office I ran into trouble. I was carpeted and castigated by Lang, The CO — an observer without either experience of piloting an aircraft or the operation of the engine instruments — for the action I considered I had prudently taken. Lang was lustily supported by Lieutenant Housser in his tirade. He asserted that the reason for the overheating was because I had closed the cooling gills. I had not done so. There was no evidence of anything being set wrongly when the aircraft was inspected at Twatt. Housser was not flying the aircraft. He was not fitted to express any opinion. Nevertheless, being a self opinionated and bombastic character he did so forcefully. I recall that he got his own way with Stephens, the solid uncompromising CO of 833 Squadron, obtaining extended leave and was even airlifted from Machrihanish to Ayr. How much easier for him to overwhelm the leader of 835 Squadron.

Is there a mental hang up, should a person in an inferior position be privy to ones progress and behaviour in an earlier period, that can cause an unjustified resentment? I opine that there might be.

Housser had trained with me at Kingston, he a Lieutenant and I but a killick. I emerged from our ITS and ATS course and operational training in no way inferior to him in flying ability. Inexplicably, for whatever reason, except the foregoing one I have pondered over, or that he simply had to be cock of the walk, he never neglected to put in a bad word for me if it served his ego.

John Lang accepted that what Housser said was right and that I was wrong. My report on the incident was swept aside and disregarded. Presumably I was given a notional black mark.

I felt sorry for yet affronted by Lang. My impression was that the job of CO was perhaps beyond his capabilities. He therefore lacked the essential confidence and more importantly showed that he did. No doubt he did his best as he saw it but his best did naught to knit the aircrews together into a spirited, happy and efficient unit. Fortunately we did that for ourselves and got on together quite well. One misfortune for our CO was that he had no sense of humour. His youthful visage ne'er creased into a smile. A laugh was unthinkable. What a pity.

Now, over fifty years later, I feel I am able to pinpoint the exact moment that I became disenchanted with the squadron's two senior officers.

The second incident concerned us all. There being no flying because the weather was judged unsuitable, though we thought not, we were in the ready room at a loose end. I was discussing the merits of certain types of printing with Shirley, others were reading or chatting. His boredom peaking, Jack Cramp produced some cards and started up a poker school. Lang, the CO happened to look in, saw what was going on, took exception to it, called Barringer into his office and demanded that the card game cease forthwith. It was presumably prejudicial to discipline and good order. He did not storm in and say his piece but left it for Barringer to disseminate his instructions.

To occupy us with something he considered more proper and instructive, Lang produced a sheaf of papers headed with subjects upon which we were to apply ourselves and write an essay. These were handed round and received by us with silent incredulity. I recall being allocated the subject "The career of Billy Binks, Air Mechanic". We were all disgusted. To spend my time penning a meaningless essay on a subject of which I had no administrative experience rather than flying, in any sort of weather, was an insult to my whole being. Some aircrew were more militant than others. For my part, being acutely aware that I was not the CO's favourite, if he had one, I deemed it inexpedient to take a leading role. I made virtually no effort to cudgel my brains over Billy Binks. The expiration of the time allowed for writing being deemed sufficient, Lang called for the completed essays. Mine had not progressed beyond the opening paragraph. I anticipated trouble on this account but other events dismissed my fears to obscurity.

As I say, some were more rebellious than others, notably Jack Cramp and Barringer. They struck out with their literary efforts expressing severe criticism of the CO in forthright and robust terms. Lang was greatly displeased. Barringer was summoned before the presence, rounded upon for his insubordination and seriously advised that he might well be faced with a court martial. 'Barry' responded that he would welcome such action which would more fully enable him to express his sentiments regarding the running of the squadron. It was perhaps just as well that the CO did not choose to confront Jack Cramp. His penmanship was more extreme than Barringers. He was a down to earth New Zealander who in basic unambiguous terms was disposed to call a spade a bloody shovel. Lang would not have cared to bandy words with Jack. He would not relish that.

The tense atmosphere gradually subsided. Each of us thought our own thoughts. They did nothing for the CO's authority. It evaporated. This state of affairs had been reached in four months. Not surprisingly, I began to feel disillusioned, restive and frustrated. I had spent twelve months training and honing my flying skills to operational level and was raring to go. Instead it seemed as if I was in a kindergarten.

The third happening quite riled me. Lang produced assessments for the flying crews. I was regarded as "below average". This had never happened before. My reports had always been "average" or more commonly "above average" never below. I had already gleaned that the CO was not exactly my friend but this action was too much. The reasoning for his decision was ludicrous. He had determined, with Housser's assistance that Housser was "above average". This was not evident to the rest of us. All other pilots were "average" excepting me. Lang's reasoning was that the squadron must average "average". It therefore followed ipso facto that if one pilot be marked "above average" then one must be marked "below average". Anyone who had reasoned thus must have had scant regard for his operational unit and his reasoning powers, I would submit, were suspect. In my management experience I sought to encourage my staff to be above average if the application was there. Our CO an unimaginative product of Dartmouth was quite unable to latch on to that concept. Oh dear!

One small but interesting matter. I realised later that I might have given the CO a very minor amount of ammunition by being rather happy go lucky regarding the analysis of navigation exercises. My observer, without my knowledge and indeed because of my indifference, was less than honest in producing the post mortem results from the relatively few Navigation Exercises (Navexs) we did. Analysed errors mysteriously became predominantly pilot errors rather than navigator errors, with the implication that the pilot's performance was at fault. By the time that I had alerted myself to this and had decided to take a keen interest in the calculations rather than just doing my job to the best of my ability, there was a change. Jack Cramp who was senior to me submitted a request that he had his own aircraft. This was granted so I had to cede to him. My observer was given the option of staying with the aircraft and flying mainly with Jack or staying as a crew with me. I was not consulted. He choose to keep to the aircraft so we parted company.

The consequences were interesting. Jack Cramp was more voluble than I. Fierce and heated rows were to be heard between him and my 'ex', particularly over navigation. Jack's penetrative researches into analysis of exercises shifted errors dramatically into navigation faults by the observer. For my part things were different. After flying with different members of aircrew for a time rather than pairing with one observer as a crew I joined company with a newcomer Sub Lieutenant McCormick, a tall serious Northern Ireland man. He proved to be a good dedicated observer. From his first arrival he took an intense dislike to the CO. Our navigation exercise results were second to none. Additional to our results 'Mac' made it his business to check the CO's results. He found them wanting by comparison with ours. I was concerned that things might come to a head because he had the single minded persistence of Ian Paisley and was getting set to ventilate his opinions without fear or favour. As it happened he didn't get the chance. Giving assistance to put away our aircraft one dark night at Machrihanish early in '43, he trapped his forearm in between the sliding doors of the hangar, broke it and consequently left the squadron as we moved on. Mac's crewing with me and the results achieved justified the earlier expressed desire of Jack Teesdale and Barry, both good and experienced observers, to fly with me to demonstrate where the faults lay. This was achieved by Barry and Dave Newbery, October '42.

After our flat spot with Lang we continued our working up in a rather routine way without any further troubles or highlights. I recall seeing two aircraft that I had not previously experienced. One none of us had seen before. It was a Barracuda which was tucked away into a hangar and zealously guarded because it was meant to be our secret weapon. It didn't take enquiring pilots too much guile to get a glimpse of this new naval reconnaissance dive/torpedo bomber which afforded good carrier landing vision with its high wing, was enclosed against the weather and was meant to be the answer to the Navy's many problems and shortages on the TBR front. I don't think many of us were convinced that it was the complete answer but then we had no opportunity of flying the odd looking craft. I suppose many folk considered the Swordfish an odd looking craft but I felt at home in Swordfish in 835 Squadron for two and a half years. The squadron continued with them until it disbanded. It was not until the end of '44 that I flew a Barracuda. I was dismayed to discover that it could not overhaul a Dakota, though without load or equipment it could be persuaded to perform a quite presentable slow roll or loop. A Dakota couldn't do that.

My other flying adventure was when for some reason I got a lift in a Sparrow, the RAF version of the Harrow, from Hatston to Donibristle. The ungainly plane was much like a railway carriage with twin engines, a high wing and a fixed undercarriage. Passengers sat on benches facing each other along the length of the cabin and were provided with bags in which to vomit if necessary. It was! The engine noise was so great that one could only with difficulty speak and be heard by one's neighbour. I just managed without disgracing myself, though I emerged gratefully at our destination a grey shade of eau de nil. I have since discovered the main reason for my discomforture. I cannot travel sitting sideways in a car or coach without its affecting my balance, and my feeling quite unwell.

What else of Hatston? Domestically the only benefit was that of Orkney cheeses which were flat, round and soft — rather reminded me of curds and whey. We bought them and despatched them to our families through the post. Any supplements to the meagre rations civilians received were most welcome. We were catered for and lived on the fat of the land, such as it was. At least we were not short. The condition of the cheese on receipt, having been entrusted to the Royal Mail for a few days, was very hit and miss but there were no complaints. All contributions were gratefully received.

Things were rounded off by a squadron dance which Barry arranged at Kirkwall. It was a dismal ill lit venue with rotten beer and a barnyard of a dance floor — maybe the beer and dance floor overlapped. It was heavy going. A good time was no doubt by many but not all, including me. At least it was a bold effort which gave the Wrens a change from their monotonous routine in the outpost. The departure from their 'curfew' hour resulted in Barry having to brave an interview with the Chief Wren, 1st Officer Rumbelow Pearce. His charm and tact enabled him to emerge unscathed.

Though fortunate to be in the Orkneys during the summer we all felt that our spell at Hatston was quite long enough and we hankered to get to sea. There was a rumour, from whence I know not, that there was a chance of flying from the escort carrier *Activity* whose squadron was due for replacement. A change did come.

On 22nd September we were ordered to HMS *Blackcap*, Stretton, a minor establishment just South of Warrington, bordering the Manchester Ship Canal. Here, close by industrial plants, flying was to some degree inhibited. Weather conditions were poor. The atmosphere was damp and subject to mists. Barrage balloons were strung out along the canal. Accommodation was rather rudimentary being in dismal dank Nissen huts. It left much to be desired, being much inferior to the Hatston appointments.

Working up continued. Additional to the inevitable dummy deck landings, against the day when we got to sea, some navigational exercises to the South, when I flew with both Barringer and Newbery as observers and bombing exercises in Llandudno Bay, the pilots got a change. Provided with packed lunches from the mess, akin to British Rail station sandwiches, we flew down to Shropshire, Ollerton, on some days, there to do some instrument flying in Oxfords. It was our first twin engined aircraft experience. Practically all our flying was 'blind', including take offs. Presumably it was both to test our confidence and give us trust in the aircraft instruments. At midday we resorted to the country house used as accommodation for the few instructors. We consumed our dried up provisions and naturally desired a drink. We were granted a concession. In the large hearth nestled a firkin of ale from Wem Brewery. We were permitted to draw ourselves a pint, very generous the instructors were, because supplies were limited, on payment of the appropriate charge. We gratefully put our monies in the box. It was super stuff, pure nectar — not fighting ale, but quite soporific. Fortunately it did not adversely affect our flying. I reckon two pints would have done. Sadly I must report that Wem Brewery is now closed.

My navigational and instrument flying results were entirely satisfactory demonstrating that there was not a scrap of evidence to justify the CO's assessment of my competence.

There was a benefit for me in being sent to Stretton. It was but a dozen miles from my home at Urmston. Public transport between the two places was non existent. Fortunately, we did no night flying from Stretton and there were virtually no station duties outside flying activities. My forward thinking over the use of my bicycle came very much into its own. The bike had of course been airlifted from Hatston. This time it was essentially for my exclusive use and no exceptions. Whilst the local pub, the *Appleton Thorn*, became the off duty centre for squadron members generally, I eschewed it and became somewhat anti social. I took opportunities to cycle home, stay overnight and return early in the morning. After all, I'd got a girl friend. I guess that I must have travelled without lights — can't remember having any. I remember particularly the early mornings, riding through misty autumnal country lanes with cheeks rosy from the frost, no doubt a bit fitter that had I been carousing in the pub.

My homing instincts were soon suppressed. On 26 October we were off again, this time for Machrihanish. No cycling home from there. Still I got home for my birthday on 19th October!

Chapter 8 — Itinerants — All at Sea

No sooner had we packed up and moved to Machrihanish, than *Activity* loomed large on the horizon. On the 30th October came the real exercise, the long promised hope of landing on a carrier at sea in the Clyde. It was at once a satisfying yet 'heart in the mouth' experience. *Activity*'s deck was but sixty feet wide, narrower than any runway or any fleet carrier's deck. The span of the Swordfish was forty five feet six inches so there was little room for error. Seen from the air for the first time, the ship appeared impossibly small for a landing. The ship turned into wind. The signal was passed for me to land. I performed the designated circuit at about two hundred feet and headed for the flight deck. I approached under the critical eye of Lieutenant Temple-West, the best deck landing control officer ('Bats') I ever came across. We were most fortunate to do our first deck landings under his guidance. But I digress. The aircraft was in a landing attitude before I reached the stern of the carrier. My speed was sepulchrally slow. Bats made frantic signals of what I must do, immediately if not sooner, to remedy the situation. I desperately heeded them, sweated blood and, I aver, came over the roundown with naught to spare, in an attitude more akin to that of a gravid seahorse than a Swordfish doing a three point landing or, as an equestrian landlubber might describe it, a 'curvet'. Cutting the throttle was hardly necessary. I clattered down, tail wheel first, picked up an arrester wire, with the hook lowered for the purpose and came to an abrupt halt. Temple-West made gestures, somewhat impolite gestures, which suggested that he was not best pleased with my initial effort. It was probably the slowest landing I ever made. However, I'd done it without mishap. It was a start. I'd succeeded. The initial inevitable fear of failure was gone. Thereafter I gained confidence, learned the correct way for me to make an approach and thereafter looked forward to deck landings with enthusiasm. The butterflies were gone.

We had practised landings on airfields, carrier type landings that is, three point landings and hardly any forward run after touching down, but we had not thought about getting airborne. This could not be simulated on land. The carrier deck was narrow and it was essential to keep straight. On the starboard side forward was the carrier's bridge. Travelling along the centre line of the deck there was a clearance by the aircraft's starboard wing of under seven feet. The carrier turned into wind for take offs. On occasions its heading was marginally inaccurate. Accelerating from a three point attitude it took some time, dependent upon wind strength and the load being carried, before one could get the tail up. Escort carriers were not speedy vessels so that wind strength was important for the Swordfish to achieve take off speed. There were many occasions when, having left the deck and passed over the bow, that the aircraft sank towards the waves before one could gain flying speed and start to climb. Those were most anxious moments for the observer and rear gunner whose impressions must, on occasions, have been that they were not in an aircraft, but making haste through the breakers in a motor boat!

We could now apply ourselves to the real thing. In twelve days from 30th October I did sixteen deck landings on *Activity*, some carrying ballast, some carrying depth charges so that I could appreciate the different handling characteristics of the plane laden and unladen. All went well.

On 13th November, to our great satisfaction, we embarked. All was different. We were brought together as a coherent whole. On land we were spread out and were not much in touch with divisions in the service other than our own. Aboard ship it was one community from Guy Willoughby, the Captain, down. He was responsible for his ship and crew. Ashore, we seldom saw the Captain of a station. Here we rubbed shoulders with seamen, officers, navigators, engineers, torpedo officers, specialist grades, deck control officers and others and realised how much we all depended one upon the other. The wardroom was very friendly, very orderly and rather cramped, as were the officers cabins. We got used to the ship's layout from the hangar to the bridge, to companionways instead of stairs and to noise. There was always some noise going on in a ship — the engines, the sea, the wind, the vents and seemingly endless pipes signalling watches and the many other orders. The greatest assault on the ears was if one happened to be just below the flight deck The sick bay was situated there and my thoughts turned to casualties being close by means of sustenance, when an aircraft landed. As the plane touched down and the hook engaged an arrester wire, the hydraulics operated and made a piercing screaming sound across the resonant metal deck surface. The operation of the single lift was a noisy and tricky procedure. Here noise was essential to warn crew members to beware of the open lift shaft. Ranging and stowing of aircraft was a skilled job. Firm securing of an aircraft below against the movement of the ship in inclement weather was very important. Everything that was done aboard ship was important. We learned quite a lot.

I was warming to our new life at sea when I found that I was more involved than I had bargained for. It came as quite a shock. Surveying the notice board, I discovered that I had been given a duty — that of Officer of the Watch. It was quite unexpected.

Commissioned flying officers were executive officers. They wore no distinguishing colour on their sleeve rank markings. They merely had an 'A' in the loop of their lace. Engineers had a maroon stripe, specialist officers green, medical officers red and so on. These were non-executive officers. They did not fall to do duties such as OOW. At sea, seaman officers were in control of the ship, but in harbour duties spread, I was soon to learn, to other officers.

Whilst training in the Clyde, carriers came close inshore overnight unless exercising, sometimes by Rothesay or Brodick Bay or more commonly by The Tail of the Bank off Gourock. On the night of my duty, between midnight and morning it was most unpleasant. *Activity* was anchored by the Tail of the Bank. I reported to the bridge, a place I'd ne'er been before to set foot on and reported to the Navigating Officer. Once up aloft I discovered it to be very dark, wet and stormy. The rain lashed down almost horizontally. I was advised of the bearings of certain key lights, reference to which at regular intervals would indicate that the ship was secure and she had not dragged her anchor. There was little else that I was told. The Navigating Officer went below and I was alone — very alone.

The wind strengthened to gale force, the tide turned. The ship swung. Various items of floating debris rushed by the ship's side on the mounting waves. The bearings I had been given, changed. The rain pelted down so that I, unfamiliar with the use of the equipment on the bridge, was far from certain as to what was going on. Presumably nothing was amiss. Flotsam still floated by so I assumed that the ship must be holding. My thoughts turned to my responsibility for all the souls aboard the carrier. Here was I, without the ability to determine if anything be amiss and ignorant of what to do if it were, except to call for help. You will recall that my total instruction on seamanship, which mostly related to knots and flags was condensed into the six weeks spent at *St Vincent* in Gosport. It was interlarded with drill, firearms, morse and semaphore, airmanship, theory of flight, navigation, how to keep and present my kit and to scrub mess tables. A sad omission from the course was how to proceed should an aircraft carrier drag anchor in a full gale. The trust vested in me for the lives of the crew of *Activity* began to bear heavily upon me.

The weather worsened and became really bad. I struggled to reassure myself that all was well. I thought it was. Was it? I had almost reached the point of seeking help, when I was released from my tortures. The Navigating Officer, observing the intensity of the gale, decided that it would be prudent if he took over the watch. He appeared beside me on the bridge. His confident manner comforted me and I gratefully handed over my responsibilities to him. I wondered at his confidence and expertise and neglecting to tell him of my fears and my incompetence, I was not disgraced.

Simulated attacks upon the ship by our aircraft, high dive bombing, anti submarine bombing, exercises homing in on targets in the ranges off the coast were included in our activities from the carrier. During our initial deck landings single aircraft were landing unencumbered by other aircraft in the vicinity. The squadron being embarked, several aircraft might be airborne together. I should therefore mention the barrier.

The carrier's deck was a little over five hundred feet long. Four arrester wires were evenly spread across it a determined distance forward of the roundown, the stern of the deck. They lay flat or appeared to do so, unless one ran along the deck without watching where one put one's feet. They were raised by metal supports each side of the deck to engage the aircrafts trailing hooks when they were landing. The bridge was situated about a quarter of the decks length abaft the bow above the catwalk, its port side flush with the starboard side of the flight deck. Abaft the bridge was the barrier, a metal mesh construction supported, when in use, by two substantial stanchions. In appearance I would liken it to a badminton net. It was for safety and protective purposes. If the deck was clear and only one aircraft was being received, the barrier was not used. If more than one aircraft was landing, or there were aircraft parked on the deck forward of the bridge, it was raised. Should an aircraft crash on landing or miss the wires and remain on the deck it was held by the barrier. The barrier also prevented damage being done to parked aircraft. Should an aircraft be waved round again by BATS and the pilot failed to clear the top of the barrier with his aircraft's hook it was a different story. The hook once lowered could not be retracted.

Barrier or no barrier, by 26th February I had twenty five safe landings to my credit. Now for some action.

To our utter dismay and disbelief we did not proceed into the Atlantic there to protect our much harassed merchant shipping. *Activity* was abruptly diverted to be deployed as a training carrier and 835 Squadron, much deflated, returned to Machrihanish. We were profoundly fed up. Exercises continued in a desultory way. We were getting muscle bound — the most worked up squadron in the Navy.

I got a change. It was the normal practice for flying officers to be made responsible for a job outside flying duties. Mine had been that of 'Aircraft Recognition Officer'. It was neither easy nor satisfying. Nobody wished to take part in recognition tests or listen. They found it boring and regarded my efforts to interest them as an irritant. My total contribution, it seemed to me, was to display prints of aircraft silhouettes on the wall of the Squadron Office. As one might well expect, the posters I was able to obtain were mainly of aircraft we were highly unlikely to come across. Instead of this activity, or non activity, I was made 'Safety Equipment Officer'. I don't recall the squadron having one before I took it on. My responsibility was for the safety equipment of the squadron, which covered parachutes, dinghies, Mae Wests and the attendant bits and pieces that went with them, such as fluorescence markers and escape kits. It was my duty to advise and instruct aircrews on the use and operation of the equipment. In this they were more interested than in the aircraft recognition. I was the expert in the field. The only omission was that I had received no instruction on the equipment myself and nothing had been arranged to that end. Representations to the CO produced nothing. On the squadron strength we had a parachute packer 'Dicky' Bird — probably an appropriate name for his calling packing 'chutes. He was not the most forthcoming individual, had something of an idle streak and was unwilling or unable to advance my knowledge on safety equipment generally. I managed as best I could by being enquiring of my new member of staff without great success. One of my first concerns was not losing our stock of parachute bags. These were zipped bags with handles, almost cube in shape, made out of robust gabardine type fabric and singularly suitable for officers to misappropriate to their personal use. Damn nuisance it was. I'd found another way to be unpopular! The solution I devised was to mark and number the bags very clearly with white dope to render them readily recognisable. I became quite proficient as a sign writer in my efforts to keep tabs on them. It worked.

For reasons not disclosed nor ever discovered, unless it was to give the officers and their staff more and more experience in shifting stores and equipment about ad nausiam, the squadron was moved after three weeks. This time our home was across the water in Northern Ireland. Kirkiston, a disused airfield, satellite to the RAF Station of Ballyhalbert, was the forlorn spot. It's facilities were rudimentary with damp nissen huts and bedding and indifferent food. The officer in charge was an RAF, non flying, Squadron Leader, who must have been as surprised at our advent as we were. I have been mild in my criticism of the station. It was quite unprepared for occupation. There was a nasty outbreak of enteritis and cleansing oneself was difficult with our appointments. The only bath, remote from our huts, in a dismal unlit brick structure, had a duckboard and virtually no hot water. Nought else. What served as a wardroom was a cheerless place. Had we been banished to Kirkiston as a penance, the place could not have been better chosen.

The squadron members knew what they wished to do. It was not hanging about in the back of beyond when there was important work to do elsewhere. Frustration was high and our daily routine did nothing to dispel it. Being the end of the year, the weather was cold and miserable. There was no life nearby, so other diversions were sought.

It was at Kirkiston that I teamed up with MacCormick. 'Mac' was conversant with the area had relatives round about. On some occasions when we were unable to fly and permitted to do so, I walked out with him. That kept me lively because he was over six feet tall, long legged and a brisk walker. I could scarce keep up with him. He led me to a small cafe, hardly recognisable as such, after a longish walk, where some sort of griddle scones were cooked. These were regarded by Mac as something of a delicacy. I must confess that it was closer to an elegant afternoon tea as compared to the mess.

One sporting venture upset the flying crews. Barry arranged a soccer match between the Officers and The Rest on Boxing Day. It was held on an inhospitable, frosty footstamping ground. At half time there was no score, the officers surprisingly holding their own. Then a loud explosion, a mid air crash and a fighter pilot from Ballyhalbert baling out of his plane. We all gazed skywards to see the pilot falling to his death, his tangled parachute trailing unopened behind him.

I felt all eyes were on me, the Safety Equipment Officer. Heart went out of our team and we lost comprehensively to The Rest.

Other diversions were sought to relieve the boredom. There was no local transport so some nights permission was granted by the CO to use our only vehicle, a clapped out Ford Utilicon, a wretched thing which invariably had to be pushed to start. 'Taffy' Jones was the only person permitted to drive — an interesting bit of misplaced trust on Lang's part there. I recall being in the back of the vehicle one night, stone cold sober, with Taffy, who was absolutely stoned, driving although he could not see. Johnny Hunt sat alongside him telling him when to turn. I should explain that Taffy, a sturdy barrel chested South Walian, needed three men to hold him in his cups. Mild as a lamb he was normally. Nothing would persuade Taffy to relinquish the driving seat. Strangely we returned to base over dark country lanes without damage to van or occupants — only to my state of mind. I avoided such trips thereafter.

A group of officers got into playing cards, including poker. Bob Selley and Jack Teesdale were keen. The quiet amiable middle aged 'Penguin' Squadron Leader was regarded as a fair cop. He was enticed to join the school after our evening repast. The intention was to clean him out. They regretted the move, because he proved to be a cunning old fox, more astute and experienced than they. He profited from the invitation whenever encouraged to join in. He, being in that sense glad of the company, the school made clandestine arrangements so as to exclude him.

There was a romantic element in the squadron. We could croon like Bing, Harmonise like the Ink Spots, smarm like Hutch and "pitch woo", as Jimmy Urquart put it. We reckoned that we were 'with it'. There were many lovely girls at Ballyhalbert. Our popularity with them was equalled by our unpopularity with the RAF boys. Perhaps they liked the black uniforms with the gold accessories. Over Christmas and New Year there were some dances which we could and did attend. I went along to the New Year's Eve dance, being implored by Johnny Hunt to oblige him by looking after a friend of his newly found young lady WAAF, Beth. I went along and felt like a spare part. That is, until I was introduced to Beth's friend, Kay. Kay was really beautiful, the music was great, the night clear with a moon like a balloon. We got on famously, had a romantic but in no wise an improper evening. We parted with no suggestion of another meeting. Jack Cramp was spending his evenings with a very lively tomboyish girl who was friendly with Kay. Each night, or early morning, he returned from his courting, he brought a long letter for me from Kay. Though I had spent but one evening with her she had fallen deeply in love with me. Eventually I had to see her, ask her not to write and put me out of her mind. We'd had a lovely evening but that was all. I felt much upset that she appeared so distressed.

There was something of a kick in the tail from seeing the girls. Beth, Kay and Jack's girl friend, whose name I cannot remember, had principal parts in a station pantomime at Ballyhalbert. As a special consideration to 835 Squadron, it was decided to give an extra show at Kirkiston. Just before the performance, the girls appeared outside our mess where they implored us to supply some Dutch courage to them in the way of a drink before they performed. Such was Jack's girl's insistence that, with my reluctant agreement, Jack obtained some Scotch but, being a generous guy, was perhaps a little too liberal with the libations. Either that or the girls were not used to it. The consequences on stage during a dance sequence were disastrous.

The Group Captain from Ballyhalbert attended the pantomime at Kirkiston and made a complaint. Jack and I, inevitably it was me again, were carpeted by Lang who did his stuff about behaviour prejudicial to good order and discipline etc and the serious consequences we faced for deliberately rendering the two WAAFs drunk. I expected him to work round to a court martial but Jack smartly chipped in said that we had given the girls one drink each on their request and that in our opinion, a small one. Lang retracted, said something about the accusation against us being deformation of character and we left him.

Other officers found themselves really involved in affairs. One fairly senior member, being more entangled than others, found himself doing the honourable thing and marrying a WAAF with whom he had been too romantic — messed up his life quite considerably, though it was, not without difficulty, brought to a reasonably harmonious solution years later. The pitfalls awaiting idle hands!

Our stay in Kirkiston, we left for Machrihanish on 29 January '43, did the CO little good. He was at an outpost, the senior naval officer in the place, was seemingly under criticism and appeared to have lost control of his squadron. We had the feeling that, although Machrihanish was overcrowded, some official decided that it would be most desirable that we be found room there. We moved back to find that our "reputation" had preceded us. Normally 835 stormed into Machrihanish and the Wrens applauded our full bloodied approach. This time we got the 'frozen mitt'. 835 had a buoyant spirit, but it had taken a battering. It took a little time for us to bounce up again, bit we did. How we desired to put that spirit to good purpose.

The year 1943 was almost unbelievable in its unsettling of the squadron. In eleven months we exceeded that in moves — a baker's dozen! As I had a personal course away from the others, I made it fourteen. There were however some interesting experiences to recall.

Being back at Machrihanish, I remembered to be careful. For some reason, in November '42, Jimmy Urquart and I had to fly over to Prestwick and return. There were just the two of us and two planes — no observers. Maybe we were collecting some thing. When we espied the runways at Prestwick we were surprised at their immense size. I called to Jimmy over the RT and suggested that we do a formation landing. He agreed. We closed up and performed a beauty, turning off the runway at the first intersection. Having completed our business there and, flushed with our success, for good measure we did a formation take off and a 'split arse' turn, once airborne, on to our heading for Machrihanish. We were received there non too cordially — were required to report to the Air Watch Office for a rollicking, an official complaint having been made by Prestwick control. We couldn't see that we had done anything amiss. We'd even spent a minimum time on their precious runway. Prudently we meekly took the dressing down and no further action ensued.

Returning to February '43 and the constant rigour of training routines — we looked for diversions. Taking an idea from 'TM', the RAF Training Memoranda mag, which we used to see, I painted an engine panel on my aircraft panel with

'Bounder', Pilot Officer Prune's wire haired terrier. It appealed because I had such a dog back home. This resulted in my receiving commissions from other pilots. Most of the aircraft blossomed out in colour. Disney characters were the most popular. 'Clara Cluck', 'Horace Horsecollar', the Dwarfs and, very appropriately for a Swordfish, the Tortoise. The CO did not apply, but showed no sign of disapproval.

We nearly lost a crew during our first bit of flying. Six of our aircraft had taxied out to fly and were on the perimeter track awaiting our turn to proceed onto the runway, when the behaviour of a Blackburn Skua attracted our attention. Having just taken off, it described a low left hand circuit and, completing it, at once came in to land. The performance was disconcerting because the aircraft with undercarriage still down aimed to make a speedy three point landing, the points being the nose of the plane and its wheels. Observing that I might be in the pilot's path if I taxied forward, I stopped dead. Housser, with Barry, in the plane ahead of me, moved forward out of the way as he sincerely hoped. The Skua made the anticipated three point landing short of Hank's plane. The radial engine broke from its formers and bounced forward flying over Hank and Barry and coming to rest in the middle of the airfield. The now inverted Skua, such of it as remained, slithered forward and smashed in to the tail of the Swordfish behind Barry's observers cockpit, its pilot held by his harness virtually unscathed, but deathly white. Mac and I had a front seat view of the action. We had not seen the like of it before. Fortunately, though two aircraft were very bent, the Skua beyond repair, nobody was injured.

I have witnessed many seemingly minor crashes which proved to be fatal. The Skua one looked like certain death. It wasn't.

My crewing with McCormick came to an end early in February. In helping to manoeuvre our Swordfish, which had gone unserviceable one dark night, into a hangar, he trapped his arm in the sliding door gear and broke it. He was off flying and because we moved on, he was off the squadron. I therefore flew with a range of observers until Taffy Jones left in April.

I did get an unexpected trip during February being sent to the carrier *Furious* to pick up two of their crew and bring them ashore. This was a new experience for me. The *Furious* was an interesting old lady being converted from cruiser to carrier in 1917. She was making smoke, quite inadvertently, when I landed and when I took off and the vessel seemed to me to be making steam from every joint in her piping. At least we spanned the years because my Swordfish updated the Sopwith Pup which first graced her deck.

I did quite an instructional trip with Jackie Parker. He was a most amiable and likable observer. We were to proceed to the bombing range at Skipness there I was to demonstrate my skills. Skipness was North of Kilbrannan Sound which separated the East of Kintyre from the Isle if Arran. To reach there one simply flew East from Machrihanish over Campbeltown, six miles distant and then North up the Sound. I didn't. Short of Campbeltown I turned North East to cut a corner aiming to drop into Ardnacross Bay. That was simple. I'd done it before. This time it was different. To my dismay, I descended from a clear sky into thick cloud. Here was a problem. Where the cloud base was I didn't know. Arran lay somewhere ahead. That was dangerous — an inhospitable landing place. The aircraft we were flying was a spare. Its engine was great, but it was neither prepared or checked for operational flying. We knew not its imperfections but we found one. We resolved to turn about, climb and fly West coming down to the West of Kintyre, then proceed North to Tarbert and come into Skipness from the North. We flew for some time and I reduced height gingerly looking down for the sea. Jackie peered over the side for the same purpose. A shout from J— "Land" —and I thrust the throttle forward and climbed. A decent period and we followed the same procedure. The same situation obtained. Up we went again. Another spell westwards and I let down gently again. This time we saw the coastline. To our disbelief we were close to the small isle of Cara just off Ardminsh, over ten miles north of our anticipated landfall or is it seafall? As I say, it was instructional. I realised how important it was that compasses were properly swung and adjusted. I also learned that clouds, especially cumulus, do not necessarily behave in a predictable fashion.

A sad note was that Jackie left the squadron a couple of months later to join a night fighter squadron. A month or two later he lost his life.

I still chuckle at this episode. Jack Teesdale was furious. I was not best pleased but not so hopping mad as Jack. He was a jolly good observer. A most capable fellow who believed in direct action. He sought some.

We'd been sent out on 'special duty'. We were to fly to Loch Fyne there to give guidance to the Army. Commandos trained there. They were to be familiarised with all UK aircraft so that they would readily be able to distinguish friend from foe. Right up my street you might say. All locally available types of planes from RAF and Navy joined in a sightseeing parade. Jack had merely come for the ride. What upset us most was the reaction of the Khaki mob when they saw our Swordfish fly past. Admittedly we were the slowest of the aircraft but they need not have made such gestures. Initially we thought it was 'V' for Victory but, being the reverse of that hand semaphore, we realised it was not. Had they not heard the fable of the tortoise and the hare?

To my surprise, on our return we were called upon to give the commandos further experience. This time no other planes were involved. I was to 'buzz' them at night whilst they were afloat in their landing craft. What a heaven sent opportunity to turn the tables. A moonlight night with about six tenths broken cloud cover gave perfect conditions to make the most of it. Jack, looking like the devil incarnate, except that his horns must have been folded back inside his helmet, joined me for the night flight. He loaded up with miscellaneous verey cartridges and off we went.

It was a great night for flying. I could see the ground and the surface of the loch but those in the landing craft could not so readily see us. We had an enjoyable time low flying for fun — really low flying. I dipped down over the craft so that the occupants had to crouch down out of our way. The soldiers did not make the same gestures as those they made in daylight. They covered their heads with their hands as though cowering under an attack. Behind me was my demon king observer firing off cartridges left right and centre. He used them all up and we returned to base secure in the knowledge that we had preserved the dignity of our beloved Swordfish.

Back in the wardroom over a celebratory Scotch, we agreed that we had really enjoyed our unexpected night out. There wasn't a lot to do in Machrihanish of an evening unless there was a dance on the station.

Humdrum activities continued into April when, as I noted, Taffy Jones moved on and I made a crew with Stan Thomas, 'Tommy'. He was a diminutive fellow from Liverpool, all of five foot two, a sincere religiously minded man with whom I had an instant rapport. The saying — "There never was a little fellow but God made it up to him some other way" was certainly apposite in Tommy's case. Bob Tidman, our TAG, completed our little company. We were an all Lancashire crew from Manchester, Liverpool and Blackpool respectively. In next to no time we were getting along fine.

Chapter 9 — Into Action and out Again

No sooner had we got organised we were overjoyed to be ordered to embark on the escort carrier HMS *Battler*. The vessel was American built and converted from a merchant craft into a carrier by scooping out the hold to be a hangar and putting a wooden top on for a landing deck. Add lifts to raise and strike aircraft, a bridge starboard forward, and that was it. *Battler*, about five hundred feet long, had a wide deck which gave more tolerance for landing. The poor welded construction proved to be inadequate to stand fierce Atlantic storms. 'Woolworth' carriers they were deservedly called. Appointments below deck were a revelation. Cabin appointments were perhaps over indulgent with most adequate storage, a writing bureau with combination safe, comfortable bunks and good lighting. All furniture was metal construction.

On 10th April, I flew aboard and settled in a well situated cabin with Robin Shirley-Smith. Cabins were allocated by seniority. Seniority in the Navy was all. Shirley's seniority and our compatibility, which caused him to request that I bunked in with him, rewarded me with a first choice berth. The place was brand spanking new and everything seemed to work.

The officially approved press got aboard whilst the ship was in harbour in the Clyde. The result was a ludicrous picture — Captain Stephenson in his best uniform; 'Wings', Major Bird, in a sidcot; another officer wearing a metal helmet, a couple of flying crew members both improperly and differently attired; some flight deck personnel congregated on the lift forward by the bridge, all represented in the print out as being actively engaged 'on the job'. I was not required in the mannequin parade.

A smart bit of working up to some purpose followed our embarkation — day and

A Swordfish landing on HMS *Nairana*. Note the narrowness of the deck area and the two Swordfish with folded back wings near the bow.

In the lower photograph, 'Bats' can be seen on the left hand side, half way along the flight deck.

night landings, live depth charge dropping, firing practice — both front and rear guns. I even got a trip to another carrier, HMS *Argus*, within the month. I felt quite a seasoned naval aviator.

The Kirkiston experience of witnessing a death, through what appeared to be a faulty parachute, stiffened my resolve that our arrangements be spot on. I searched through *Battler* for a place to pack our 'chutes. Persistent harassing of the ship's Commander, a martinet of an officer of short stature and temper, whose name I have forgotten, resulted in his reluctantly providing some space in the bow beneath the flight deck. It would just suffice. My packer confirmed that he could manage there. A table was provided after more repeated requests and, having as he thought, met my needs, the Commander summoned me to inspect the chippies handiwork. He was obviously glad to be free of my representations. He also, through his manner, made it clear that I was a probationary acting temporary Sub Lieutenant RNVR, whereas he was a Commander RN. A packing table had been provided after much trouble and inconvenience. That was that. He wished to hear no more.

I surveyed the table. Its length and width was correct. Its surface was not. The top was as rough as a vegetable grater. A silk parachute drawn over it would have been shredded to ribbons.

I recall once presenting a piece of rough planed mahogany to an upholsterer of my acquaintance with a request that he polish it. This brought a swift response. Inspecting the wood, he looked doubtful and ejaculated, "It's like a bear's arse," adding, "—trade term Mr Sadler," by way of explanation for his use of the vernacular. My reaction to the surface of the table equated to the upholsterer's reaction to the mahogany. My knowledge of parachute packing left me in no doubt that a smooth lino type surface was essential atop the coarse wood. I said so, being careful not to lapse into a colloquialism.

That did it. A Subbie did not contradict a Commander. A storming row ensued in which I had the temerity to advise my senior officer that his knowledge of flying crews safety equipment was deficient. He no doubt understood ships but not aircraft. He was most displeased and said that I could not indent for the material I required and, indeed, if permitted to do so, I would not get it. He stormed off.

My action was precipitate. By devious means, I indented for what I regarded as essential without delay. I suppose that I must have been protected by some unseen benign spirit. I was not demoted. I was not even reported..

To my surprise, the order was executed with despatch. The remarkable thing was that the thirty foot roll of lino was six feet wide, not three as ordered. My packer and I quickly surfaced the table and we were in business. I secured the unexpected bonus of surplus lino out of sight of prying eyes. Fortunately, the Commander had no intention of having anything further to do with Sadler or parachutes and, to the best of my knowledge, completely excluded our parachute packaging den from his rounds. We were well pleased with our table and we checked the 'chutes.

Having acquired a splendid strip of lino, I guarded it carefully. It was transferred

HMS *Battler.*

form base to base under my eagle, or was it evil eye? I had intentions for its use. Alas, when getting from ship to shore close to my home it strayed. It was obviously close to somebody else's home! I was in the air party. I entrusted my prize to my stores PO (I had by then become Stores Officer) I saw it no more. It no doubt found a welcoming home somewhere in the UK.

To polish off our preparedness we were disembarked to RAF Ballykelly for a fortnights intensive 'Western Approaches' course. War games were played with models so that we might learn the tactics adopted by our ships and aircraft and the function of Western Approaches Command in Liverpool where monitoring of all ship and aircraft movements were fastidiously maintained. Alerted to the techniques and anticipated rigours of combating the U-boat menace we completed our course well informed and ready for action.

Creature comforts at Ballykelly were few. Damp nissen huts compared unfavourably with the luxury of *Battler's* appointments and food.

I must relate one incident, amusing to me, which illustrates the disparate characters of 835 Squadron members.

Stan Thomas, my observer, and I had turned in. Our accommodation I have described. Rudimentary it was. We made ourselves as comfortable as possible and eventually managed to get off to sleep.

In the early hours of the morning we were disturbed by the return of Bob Selley and Charlie Cross, two inebriated pilots, from their roistering alcoholic outing. They burst into our hut, presumably being uncertain of theirs. Bob was particularly noisy as he usually was having drunk half a pint any night. He was in fierce argument with Charlie over the relative merits of contraceptives. Tommy and I were not pleased and said so. Tommy, a straight and very proper religious man had had enough. He got out of bed and drew himself up to his majestic five feet two, arrayed in his blue and white striped pyjamas. He remonstrated with the intruders to no avail.

Charlie draped his arm over Tommy's shoulder in an avuncular manner and asked "Tell me Tommy, what do you think of french letters?" Tommy by now quite indignant retorted, "I'll have nothing to do with them". "There you are", said Charlie. "I told you. He's a Rendells man". That did it! Tommy was exceedingly cross. For my part, I found the scene so funny that, in spite of my annoyance with the two of them, I just burst into laughter.

I got rid of them by throwing them out. I got no thanks from Tommy. He took me to task for seeing any humour in such a disgraceful performance. But then, as John Cridland remarked in '91, recalling us as we were in '43, "I always remember the two of you — Stan so serious and you so jokey".

Our Western Approaches course completed, we repaired to HMS *Gannet*, Eglinton, near Londonderry. Here was a good compass base for calibrating our equipment. In less than a week the call came for action. The squadron had to be temporarily divided. Three Swordfish had to remain at Eglinton under Robin Shirley-Smith. The other six, including me and mine had to fly to Sydenham, near Belfast, be taxied to the docks, an odd experience and hoisted aboard *Battler*, an even odder one. We were to join a Gibraltar bound convoy out of Liverpool off Rathlin Island. The reason for our depleted squadron became obvious when we embarked. *Battler* was sailing in not just a protective capacity, but was also ferrying Spitfires and equipment to Gibraltar in preparation for the Allied invasion of Italy. Spitfires did not have folding wings hence room in the hangar was at a premium.

My first anti submarine patrol was on 6th June. At last I was active. The outward convoy was uneventful in clement weather. I continued patrols as I was detailed. I presumed that our constant activities kept enemies away.

I say the voyage was uneventful. It was until we were just of the Rock. The Spitfires had to be got ashore. We had some RAF personnel aboard to fly them. 'Wings' devised his plan to do this. Swordfish were brought on deck to make room to manoeuvre the fighters in the hangar. Their wings were folded, then they were parked from the stern forward along the extreme edge of the flight deck. This reduced the effective take off width of the deck, but it was deemed to be sufficiently wide for the Spitfires to manage reasonably comfortably. At least, Wings, our Marine Major, thought so. I found myself having the temerity to assume the role of Cassandra in addressing my concern to him. His attitude was quite unperturbable. His response, oft on his lips, was "Pooh Bah. All Serene". I might have been in Tittipu. It felt like it. Within but a few minutes one pilot, in taking off, slewed to port before he reached the bow of the ship probably being intimidated by the bulk of the

Swordfish lined up along the flight deck of HMS *Battler* off Gibraltar. On the right, a Spitfire can just be seen shrouded in the smoke from the ship. This photograph was taken shortly after another Spitfire had crashed into the sea on take off.

bridge looming to starboard. The aircraft struck a gun in the port catwalk, plunged into the sea. We saw aircraft and pilot no more. I tried to resolve to keep my thoughts to myself. They were deep.

We got some ten days at Gibraltar and spent time ashore. It was most pleasant to be able to walk through the labyrinth of tunnels through the Rock to he Mediterranean side and Sandy Bay, where we officers were permitted to swim and sunbathe in off duty hours. Being interested in visiting Spain, I obtained a visa having first gathered together some scruffy civilian clothes and had my photograph taken. I sought advice from the MO. He was a huge man, very bad on his legs. He counselled that I should drink no water, consort with no females — otherwise enjoy myself. One other thing, wear some headgear. Very friendly and fatherly to me he was. Wine, he said, was the thing to drink.

I crossed the land border to La Linea and attended a bull fight with some other officers. Not understanding the skills required and feeling that things were loaded against the animals, we cheered the bulls to the disapproval of the local populace. Another day I crossed by ferry to Algeciras and attended another bull fight. On this occasion I found myself sitting alongside an erudite Spaniard who spoke good English. He explained the virtues of a first rate matador and described the moves made in the ring. I realised that, from his information the La Linea performance was much superior to the one we were witnessing as every wrong or ugly movement was pointed out to me. I suppose one might enjoy bull fights from a purely technical point of view if well informed, but I did not warm to it at all. Returning on the ferry, pitching our empty wine bottles into the sea like the unkempt vandals we resembled, I looked out West to the Spanish mainland. I knew that a vantage point in the hills was a lookout post from which Gibraltar was clearly visible. Information, gleaned from constant observation, was passed on to our German enemies. It was a disconcerting thought that a timetable of convoys leaving the Rock was posted daily to the constant danger of our shipping.

Sunshine in the Med' was different to sunshine in the UK. It was a new experience for me and for others. Although there was cloud over the Rock and we therefore felt safe from sunburn we were wrong. Among others I was foolish enough to get myself burned from over-exposure and I returned to *Battler* one day quite sore. My discomfort increased when I found myself with more trouble, because I itched all over. The MO diagnosed Scabies and prescribed the cure — standing under a shower with a stiffish brush, scrubbing the offending insects out of the angry raised spots. That was the nearest I got to Hank Housser, he having the same symptoms as I. We stood in adjoining showers, both in extreme discomfort. Scrubbing out parasites from a tender sunburnt body by being harsh enough to cause the spots to bleed was a self flagellating experience. Mind you the doc' was right. It worked.

During our stay in Gib' I was invited over to another carrier, HMS *Ravager*, which was on the same mission as we were. She was ferrying Grumman Wildcats. Because it was Sunday the menu was roast pork and all the trimmings, in spite of our sweating freely in an airless mess below decks. I gathered that the lower deck would riot if the Sunday meal was varied, regardless of conditions. I heard a familiar voice. The dulcet tones of Stephens my erstwhile CO in 833 Squadron assailed me. He was now a Lieutenant Commander, 'Wings' on *Ravager*. He was complaining bitterly about being unable to fly an aircraft. I eavesdropped, not difficult at fifty yards with Stephens. In USA, from whence *Ravager* had sailed, the US Air Force had given Stephens a Hellcat. Unbelievable but true — just gave him one! He wished to fly it. I went over to his table, introduced myself and put a suggestion to him. "Bloody good idea", he said. When the Wildcats were off loaded the Hellcat somehow got confused with them as I had suggested, so that he'd got his precious gift ashore. He flew the craft with gay abandon round the Rock and into the Western Med'. Finding a Miles Master on the airfield I requested of Wings that I might fly it. I was told there were dangerous air currents round the promontory and was resolutely refused permission. Of course I was but a Sub Lieutenant.

The brief holiday was soon over and we put to sea again escorting a homeward bound convoy. My thoughts strayed to the Spanish air watch office and movements recording bureau. I could envisage wires buzzing as our departure was signalled. Shortly after getting underway our radar picked up an enemy aircraft. Two Seafires were sent off to intercept. This they did most efficiently shooting down the Focke Wulf Condor which was attempting to shadow us. That danger removed the aircraft could not signal our position and course to the U-boats as intended. We proceeded with the voyage acutely aware of the unseen perils of the Bay of Biscay. Many U-boats lurked there. Constant patrols by our Swordfish kept the submarines under water. If they surfaced their sea to air detectors would pick us up and we could spot them, so for safety they had to submerge and were unable to track or keep pace with the convoy. There was something of a lack of satisfaction for the TBR pilot in that he could not see what he had achieved. Scanning miles of featureless sea was monotonous but very necessary and obviously it must have saved innumerable lives. Neglecting to patrol the area round the convoy could mean disaster.

Once safely home to the UK the squadron flew off to Eglinton. Here there were changes. We found that we had become a 'combined' squadron consisting of Swordfish, as before, plus six Sea Hurricanes. There were five fighter pilots ex 804 Squadron, followed by Wilf Waller, an RN Lieutenant, converted from flying Walrus to fighter aircraft. He became the fighter section leader. On the TBR side, Housser moved to another squadron to be replaced by Eric McEwan, an Edinburgh Scot. Paddy Hall, a Northern Ireland observer also joined us.

Another interesting change from the squadron and my personal point of view, was that I had become an 'above average' pilot. Fancy that.

We spent about two weeks in Eglinton enjoying lovely weather. I went for some pleasant country walks with Shirley when off duty. The sunshine and the quiet of Derry was relaxing. It felt so removed from the war. We lay back and savoured our pipes. Shirley always had his camera to hand. The pictures produced were, of course, black and white. I have a clear memory of our jaunts in his photographs. To my surprise on visiting Katalin, his widow, in '94 (Shirley died a year or so before) I was shown several snaps of me in Shirley's album, including one in the 'all together' as I returned to our shared cabin in *Battler* after having a shower. Shirley delighted in the candid camera shot.

Getting out with Tommy was next to impossible. It taxed my patience, because he took an eternity to get ready to go out. A young lady preparing for a ball was lightning compared to Tommy. For a soccer match he could do it. He was a good player — got his blue at Oxford later. We played in some good games together for I was too keen. Quite different personalities were my friends. Shirley eschewed games. Bezique was about as far as he'd go. The other timely turn out by 'T' was a church service. We went together occasionally, probably a unique activity in 835, apart from Sunday divisions. Denomination did not much concern us, we believed in a catholic church, so long as we could sing, we could both sing well. Just the one occasion took us off balance. When attending a service in a small non conformist chapel near Eglinton, we squeezed ourselves into the choir and were presented by the minister with hymn books — with the tunes in tonic sol-fa! We had both learned our early music at elementary school by the method devised by Sarah Glover, in early 1800s and, I suppose, being a Swordfish crew we were adjudged antediluvian!

Our easy life was disturbed by our getting a new weapon — rocket projectiles. They were mounted on racks beneath the wings, four to port and four to starboard. They had armour piercing heads, no initial velocity and therefore no recoil when fired as a salvo or in pairs. A few days were spent in Machrihanish equipping the planes and in our learning how to handle them. They were intended for use against surface vessels and were extremely effective. When dropping depth charges, the Swordfish had to maintain a steady level course and a speed not exceeding one hundred and ten knots. The weapons would not perform satisfactorily otherwise.

Consequently a U-boat on the surface had a very good chance of shooting down the plane before it reached its target. The rockets put an end to that. The rockets could be released from quite a distance whilst the aircraft was in a gentle dive. They travelled so fast that the pilot could fire two, watch the result and adjust his sight if necessary before firing again, whilst in the same dive. Fired at the critically correct angle and speed, the rockets would enter the water, level out a few feet beneath the surface, speed along at a constant depth and emerge from the water still at great speed half a mile or so further on. The armour piercing heads inflicted considerable damage. A difficulty for the pilot was the positioning of the 'Mickey Mouse' as we called it, the console on which the firing sequence was selected. It was somewhere to port behind one's left shoulder blade. With the range of equipment and controls in the Swordfish cockpit, it was very difficult to get at anything with ease. I found it easier, were I to use rockets, to set the box to 'pairs', before I took off and have done with it. In any case it was the most satisfactory sequence of firing in my experience.

We embarked once more on *Battler*. In loading gear aboard there was a mishap affecting only me. My cabin trunk was accidentally dropped out of a landing net into the sea and it disappeared to a watery grave. I was advised to claim for my lost property, mainly uniform, in the approved manner on the proper form. Officers aboard, who had experienced losses, advised me to claim over and above what was lost because claims, according to them, were always cut down on principle. My submission I kept within reasonable bounds. Nonetheless, I was summoned to report to Lang, the CO. He had my document before him and had found fault with it. "Don't you know that it is against regulations to have a petrol lighter aboard an aircraft carrier?" he demanded. I was annoyed. When I won my wings in Canada, like most of the other smoking graduates, I bought a Ronson lighter with Air Arm Wings on the side of the case. I valued it, more for its sentimental attachment than anything else. It was in my trunk. I had quite properly claimed for it. This business of being carpeted by the CO was getting irksome. It was just he and I on this occasion. "My lighter was sans flint, sans wick and sans fuel. It was put away because it was not in use. Did you expect me to throw it away?" I fiercely retorted. There was no reply. My claim was accepted and signed without any amendment.

The claim irritant out of the way we settled in, did some concentrated stuff on anti submarine bombing and were ready to get to sea again.

Once more a blow fell. *Battler* was withdrawn from being an operational carrier to being a supply ship bound for Gibraltar, loaded so that there was insufficient room to operate aircraft. We were sent ashore to RAF Ayr.

It was summer. The weather was good. I had not been to Ayr before. It complemented my free naval tour of the Scottish coastline. Although we did the usual exercises, lest we lost our flying skills, we had some leisure time. I bathed in the sea, my efforts to get out of it being stretched to the limit when I discovered that I had a seal for company!

Eric McEwan and I soon became pals and spent some evenings out together enjoying a dram and some pleasant female company. We had hardly cemented the friendship before Eric nearly lost his life. Summer or not, the Clyde could quickly become angry, visibility be much reduced and conditions change from good to bad. Eric was piloting a Swordfish one evening returning to Ayr from Machrihanish with Lt Wilkinson, a pilot from another squadron, as passenger. The engine cut dead and Eric ditched the aircraft south of Arran. The Swordfish sank. The dinghy released properly but, being holed by the aircraft's damaged wing, it proved useless. Dependent upon Mae Wests to keep afloat, the two airmen struck out for Arran, the nearest land, being guided by a fire lit by a farmer who had seen the aircraft come down. An exhausted Eric made it — just. He was dragged ashore. Tragically Wilkinson didn't. He was washed up on the shore later, dead.

He had, shortly before, happily survived an unpleasant experience at Machrihanish. A new and clever method was devised by the pundits of attacking a submarine on the surface at night. We practised it. The technique was thus. Flying at about two thousand feet, a common patrol altitude, the observer picked up a contact ahead. A submarine! About two miles away or a bit closer, the pilot released a parachute flare, turned aside forty five degrees and dived, judging his descent so that he could turn in quite steeply a little above the water beyond the submarine. The flare now being illuminated, The sub' was silhouetted and the pilot could proceed with a depth charge or bomb attack. Straightforward and effective it was, if all went well.

With Wilkinson it did not go well. The night of the exercise was very dark. The 'submarine' was a floating target at Skipness, a triangular float with a pole surmounted by a substantial yellow ball. We used such targets for bombing practice. 'W' did everything precisely and correctly as did his observer. Flare dropped, dive undertaken, a steep turn to execute the 135 degree turn necessary to line the target with the flare, he had done it very well. The flare was extinguished as he banked the Swordfish just above the sea. Flying aids became useless. The artificial horizon toppled as did the gyro compass. Instantly the pilot was disorientated, quite unable to determine if the plane was straight and level. It was. The airscrew boss of the Swordfish struck the ball on the target, knocking it forward. It swung back like a kelly and cleared all the fabric from the underside of the aircraft's body beneath the observer and gunner. I saw the aircraft the following morning. Additional to a very open rear cockpit, the three metal airscrew blades were curved about a foot from their tips. Even so, the aircraft flew back, perhaps a mite roughly and landed safely. Being disenchanted with the reliability of flares, we were not overkeen on this inventive mode of attack. Let the pundits try it.

Another sad note came about this time. Bob Tidman, our TAG, home at Blackpool for leave had an accident and lost his arm — a tram collision. L/A deFraine joined Tommy and I making up our crew.

The licensing laws in Scotland were such that pubs were closed on Sundays. The

RAF station at Ayr was uninspiring so the boys preferred to go out for a drink in the evening, Sunday evening being normally a free one. An effective ruse was employed. One officer booked a room for the night. Residents could drink on the Sabbath — so could the fifteen guests he invited providing the costs were on his bill. We got away with it. Which publican would turn away good business? The lounge in the Station Hotel was comfortable and civilised and the most suitable place to spend an otherwise dull evening. I don't think the idea was repeated but then I spent some time away. My Safety Equipment course came up.

Nipping away early one Friday afternoon, my friends arranging that I was not on the pm flying programme whereas the CO was, I dodged him. Travelled via Manchester, enjoyed some brief home comforts and reported to HMS *Raven*, Eastleigh to start my course on the Monday. Pretty good going to be destined to become acquainted with the niceties of safety equipment more than twelve months after being made responsible for it! It was tedious travelling long distances by train during the war. The tedium disappeared once on the course.

Its members were about a dozen Wren parachute packer trainees, a Sub Lieutenant from 817 Squadron and me. Our instructor was a Chief Petty Officer. We started in the water. Presumably that was the correct way, being more naval. It was a jolly and diverting part of the course. We were in a swimming bath learning how to right an upturned dinghy, how to inflate it, how to get into it and so on. It was my first experience of learning some skills cavorting with a dozen lovely lasses, the rig of the day being bathing costumes. We two officers just managed to keep our minds on the job though helping course members could be distracting. Having covered the 'staying afloat' part of the instruction and having been made conversant with the operation of all aids to that end, we turned to parachutes.

After our first inspection of a parachute, it was bigger than most of us thought, there was a demonstration of packing, then another, then another. We were shown how to fold it so as to get it into its case. Our instructor showed how one straightened out a tangled 'chute. It looked impossible at first. The Wrens were then set to try packing under close guidance. A wrongly packed 'chute was a death trap. This went on for most of the session then on to the following day. I got restive and said I wanted a go. The CPO said officers on course did not pack. I informed him that this one did. I had come a'purpose. He remonstrated. I insisted. He relented and I got on with it. There was quite a technique in doing the job but I persevered, got the knack of it and soon became proficient at it. I wished to return to 835 Squadron with the ability to do all that my packer could even though I had but one week to do so.

I returned to Ayr able to advise the air crews on every aspect of safety equipment and with a good working knowledge of its care and maintenance. AB Bird, my packer was rather surprised to find that I could pack a parachute as well as he could.

We got a bit of leave, then there were some changes. The CO, John Lang, left and was replaced by Wilf Waller who was promoted to Lieutenant Commander. Also Robin Shirley-Smith moved to a shore appointment. Hoping for a change giving

HMS *Argus*. The light coloured area in the centre of the flight deck was the retractable bridge used when there was no flying activity. The other bridge, used during flying, can be seen protruding from the starboard catwalk.

some constancy from our desultory dull days, we got an unexpected one. The fighter group went to HMS *Ravager* there to perfect their deck landing ability. We TBR crews embarked on an old lady I had already visited, HMS *Argus*. She wasn't the vessel of mythology, nevertheless she was converted to an aircraft carrier in 1918.

Argus was unique. At sea she had an unobstructed level deck with no superstructure, The 'bridge' used being on the starboard catwalk. When not flying aircraft, another bridge was raised midships forrard. It looked for all the world like a small shed. She vibrated so that one could estimate her speed from the noise. At least I could, because though I was lodged in a quite generously sized personal cabin midships with no ports, I could sense what was going on in the engine room. Being amidships my accommodation was remarkably stable.

Our task was to try out the Navy's new weapon, the 'buoyancy bomb'. The bombs were designed to be dropped in a string ahead of one's target. Instead of exploding on impact, they sank. Then rose to the surface again rather like surface

H. M. S. CHASER
c/o G. P. O.
LONDON

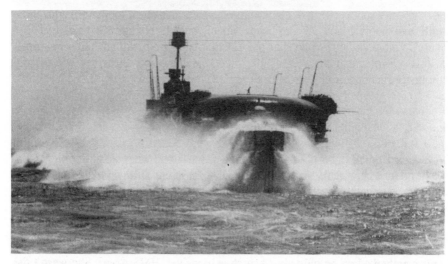

mines. We dropped them to order as directed and the inventive boffins aboard observed them without revealing their conclusions. It was something to do rather than repetitive exercises — 'hush hush' stuff it was too. Top Secret and all that. I got on well with 'Wings', Lt Cdr McTurk, and was encouraged to do plenty of flying. One day I did six landings to give a new batsman experience. Another day I ferried senior naval officers about, being on three carriers — *Argus*, *Furious* and *Chaser* in the one day. I also took three army staff officers ashore. They had come on board to check the feasibility of an Auster aircraft landing on a carrier. These aircraft were used as army spotting planes. With a landing speed of but thirty five miles per hour and a very light frame, it took an oversize deck crew to grab the plane on landing so that it was not blown overboard. I flew the officers to Ayr practically on the water because I loved flying low on the sea. I must confess that they were delivered ashore with ashen complexions having been wedged in the back cockpit for twenty five minutes. I enjoyed the flip more than they did, but they did behave a bit important.

The 14th October was my special day. I completed 100 deck landings without mishap. Nobody else in 835 Squadron achieved that. Pre-war, the RN pilots were welcomed into the 'Perchance Club' if they reached the faultless 100, but the club did not seem to exist in '43. Maybe I celebrated with a drink.

On a gastronomical note. I suppose that in '43 I was quite a trencherman if the presentation was good. On *Argus* we had no leave, but Saturday from noon and Sunday was free. Like office hours it was. On Saturday most officers made off somewhere. I didn't bother and a trip home was too far distant. How I remember the Saturday lunches. The cook produced his speciality, the best steak and kidney pudding I ever have tasted. It was an exciting epicurean experience, a mountain of pudding sufficient for so many when there were so few to dine. I freely confess that I overindulged myself, retreated to an easy chair in the commodious wardroom where I relaxed with a book, loosened my corsets and, being more than replete, was rendered supine against the time for afternoon tea. *Argus* had retained an air of comfortable living. Let others bustle about.

In early November, we were moved. This time it was to HMS *Chaser*, another Woolworth carrier. Captain McClintock welcomed us, had heard of our seemingly pointless perigrinations and said that we had now got our own carrier at last. We did the usual working up for familiarity with the carrier both night and day flying. I still got a bit of ferrying, including to *Furious*. Then, within that month, the ship was withdrawn for immediate overhaul and we were ashore to Abbotsinch thence to *Gannet* at Eglinton.

I got a new squadron job at Eglinton, that of deputy to Jack Teesdale as Stores Officer. This was a responsible job. During the squadron's existence, stores had been a constant difficulty. There had been nobody better than Jack, who used his

Facing: Top — HMS *Chaser*.
             Middle — HMS *Furious*
             Bottom — HMS *Nairana*

ingenuity, to keep things going. A notable feature was the cannibalisation of damaged aircraft. Many were damaged on landing and dependent on the severity of the accident and the storage situation in the hangar, they were either manoeuvred to the hangar for repair, or ditched. Bert Timms and Alf Gibbon, air mechanics, were expert in the miraculously swift removal of spare parts to stock our stores with the most likely call for spares. Barry, Jack and Chief Aircraft Artificer Banham worked wonders in the stores. A more acquisitive assembly one could not imagine. Jack had been in the squadron longer than I and it was desirable that he had a stand-in.

Whilst at Eglinton, Johnny Hunt once more got me entangled with the fair sex, this time quite without notice. He and I were of similar build and appearance and would roughly answer to the same description — providing one's assignation was to meet under the clock wearing a red carnation. Early one Saturday afternoon, I came out of the wardroom on my way to Londonderry to find an attractive, size one, WAAF standing impatiently outside. The young lady was turned out very smartly with rather more beauty aids than regulations permitted. Very dishy indeed she was. Seeing me, she at once chided me for being late and indicated that we should be off. She linked my arm in a most possessive manner and propelled me towards the bus stop before I could draw breath. I tried to hold back and enquired where we were going. She made it clear that we were off to 'Derry as had been arranged the previous evening — surely I had not forgotten especially after last night! I confessed that I knew nothing of last night. She was amazed, rather cross and hurt. Our most romantic interlude, she asserted, was unforgettable. Her excited enthusiasm put me in mind of the Arabian Nights. Things came to a head and my head cleared a little when she addressed me as 'Johnny'. I pointed out that I did not rejoice in the name of 'Johnny'. She assured me that I did the night before. By exhibiting my identity disc which bore my name, I sought to convince her that my name was not Johnny Hunt but George Sadler. She was loathe to believe that. It was with the greatest difficulty that I managed to disentangle myself from her close embrace and retreat to the wardroom. There I found Johnny playing cards. He was adamant that he was not prepared to emerge and face his overardent suitor. He disappointed me with his lack of gallantry but I must admit that, had he done so, the prospects would have been stormy and as I said, she was a big girl and an emotionally charged one.

I felt nervous about going out again but, following the advice given to the returning wise men, I left the wardroom by a different door and, by taking a longer circuitous route, managed to reach the bus stop unmolested. Holy writ is sometimes helpful. I felt hot under the collar until I was safely aboard the bus.

Shortly after this hazardous adventure we got some Christmas leave so I recovered my composure in the arms of my true love.

We returned from leave to what one might call a sea change in both senses. Wilf Waller moved on after his short stay with us and was replaced by Lt Cmdr JT Miller, RN who had been employed as an operational instructor on TBR aircraft at Arbroath. The great news was that an escort carrier built in the Clyde commissioned in December had a prospect of being our new home. Her name was HMS *Nairana*. Our nine Swordfish and six Sea Hurricanes under our new Commanding Officer were ready and eager to go.

Chapter 10 — A Permanent Home

On 30th December I flew aboard. *Nairana* was about 14,000 tons with a flight deck about 500 feet long, but only 60 feet wide. That gave little tolerance for a Swordfish's span was 45.5 feet. The freeboard from the deck was 46 feet. She was robustly built, but without the sophisticated comforts below decks found on the Woolworth carriers. There was one lift at the stern compared with the Woolworth carriers two — fore and aft — which made ranging and striking an aircraft a difficult and precise job, particularly so because the Hurricane wings did not fold.

The Captain, RMT Taylor RN, was a seasoned campaigner with much sea experience, but minimal flying knowledge. Commander Healey RN, a most amiable ship's commander, complete with parrot in his cabin, sometime Uncle Mac of the BBC Childrens' Hour and the Captain had been brought back into harness due to the exigency of the war. Lt Commander Godden RN, was Senior Operations Officer. Most of the other ships officers were RNVR. 'Wings' was Lt Cmdr Edgar Bibby, 'Bats' was Lt Bill Cameron and our Met' Officer Sub Lt Arrowsmith.

There was intense and urgent activity getting the ship run in and in honing our flying to perfection. We put to sea in company with HMS *Activity* and in command of Captain Walker and his six sloops of the 2nd Escort Group. On 1st February I flew my first patrol. We were hunting for submarines. They were hunting for us! Before the day was through, an urgent signal was received from one of the sloops that a submarine was about to attack *Nairana*. It had been observed at periscope depth and had penetrated the outer screen of little ships. Evasive action was taken and after a creeping attack, perfected by Captain Walker, the submarine was sunk. We were grateful for the captain's skills and reflected on the possible fate of the eight hundred souls on the carrier. We kept our patrols flying trusting that we were doing some good.

I flew a patrol on 4th February with Dalton as my observer. In the evening, my back seized up so that I could not bend. I was in severe crippling pain. It laid me low. The Medical Officer, Lieutenant Dodds, shepherded me to my bunk and applied the comfort of hot water bottles — not too efficacious. The wind had eased, but there was still a sea swell and the movement of the aircraft carrier did not help me.

I lay uneasy on my bunk in acute pain from the lumber region, conscious of the bustle of activity on the flight deck as aircraft took off and landed. Calling out for information when somebody passed my cabin, I learned that a search was on. One of our Swordfish was missing. It had not returned from a routine patrol long after its ETA. There was no evidence of enemy action. Someone told me that the missing

The coolness and trust that an observer has in his pilot is clearly shown in this photograph taken from a Swordfish immediately after take-off from HMS *Nairana*.

Swordfish crew was the pairing of Dalton and Costello. The carrier and escorts, not being on convoy duty but operating as a hunting group, course was set towards the missing aircraft's last presumed position and search aircraft were deployed without respite. It was 5th February. As I say, I, as pilot, had flown with Dalton on a patrol the previous day. My inability to join in the search irked me. To lie prone was infuriating.

Dalton, an observer, had joined the squadron as replacement crew but a short time before. Having flown in the Mediterranean he was now to experience service with

835 Squadron in the North Atlantic theatre of war. I had regarded him as somewhat conceited, cocksure and outspoken. He made himself rather unpopular with some aircrew members, possibly because of these traits.

I witnessed two fist fights in which he was engaged. One was with Elliott, a most quiet and placid pilot. Another was with Urquhart. These were the only occasions I ever witnessed or heard of officers fighting during my two and a half years in the squadron.

Dalton crewed with Costello, a very different character. He was tall, suave, laid back, a public school type — Harrow. He was also a good pilot. It was a pairing of men with disparate backgrounds and attitudes.

I recalled incidents that took place only six days earlier. Dalton was aboard *Nairana* on the present trip by pure chance and others efforts. On 26th January the squadron was at Machrihanish awaiting orders to embark on *Nairana*. Our new CO, having just been appointed, was finding his feet. Barringer, as senior observer, was aware of requirements and doing his best to see that they were met. We stood at short notice to fly aboard.

Contrary to the general edict, Dalton was permitted, due to his persistent requests, to take a forty eight hour leave on the clear understanding that he could readily be contacted and report back immediately if called. The weather deteriorated. We had heavy winds, rain and low cloud. Orders were received to embark on 28th January. Road and rail communications between the Mull of Kintyre and the mainland were cut, so that Dalton, when called, was unable to return. He was told to get himself to Ayr. There he would be uplifted by aircraft.

The weather worsened through to the 28th, our day of embarkation. We had to move. Barringer knew we were short of an observer and was also mindful that we were short of an aircraft on complement. An observer probably waited at Ayr. A replacement aircraft was available at Renfrew. It had not been collected earlier because of the inclement weather. In spite of the very bad weather conditions, Barry sought permission of Air Control to pick up Dalton from Ayr. It was refused. Things looked difficult.

Resourceful Barringer conceived a courageous but risky plan of action, which brought me as a senior and respected pilot into the frame. As the rest of the squadron were prepared and flew West to join the carrier off Rathlin Island, I flew off with Barry and carrying a pilot, Eric McEwan, eastwards to Ayr. The weather was wild, visibility almost nil. I clearly recall the conditions. Only the bottom hundred feet of Ailsa Crag could be discerned below the cloud base. We flew into the RAF Station at Ayr, found Dalton, got him aboard and set of for Renfrew, navigation being by road than ought else. We landed safely on the sodden airfield with its metal mesh covering 'gainst the mud and found a replacement aircraft, a Swordfish, close to hand. It was quickly fuelled and we took it over in haste without the formality of either signature or 700 check.

McEwan and Dalton boarded the replacement aircraft and we flew out. Mac keeping close formation with me so that we rendezvoused with *Nairana* off

Northern Ireland. Our landings complemented the squadron's strength aboard. I recall Captain Taylor's laconic "Good Show". The bold stratagem had paid off. Its failure — two aircraft, two pilots, two observers short! The consequences were unthinkable.

Painfully confined to my bunk, frustrated, uncomfortable thoughts beset me. The search continued without success.

Doc' Dodds came in to see me. He was the most caring medical officer I had ever come across during my naval service. Particularly keen on the well-being of the flying personnel, he saw to it that all had three monthly medical checks. He was conscientious, took his duties seriously and spent time getting to know the crews. That he should look in to enquire of my condition surprised me. My malady was but a transitory one, which had no bearing on my general health. No doubt I would recover in a day or two. Lieutenant Dodds was much troubled. I had not seen him so before. He felt that he must speak with somebody in his anxiety. He chose to speak to me.

He had a continuing concern, he said, in respect of the condition of Jimmy Urquhart, one of the pilots. Urquhart had, in his opinion, been drinking to excess. This Dodds attributed to the bad influence of Tony Costello, a playboy who overindulged and encouraged others to do so. He had raised the matter with Costello, but to no avail. They had not parted on the most friendly terms following his representations. Costello, in his casual manner, belittled and dismissed Dodd's genuine worries. As Dodd's express purpose in discussing the situation was the welfare of the flying crews, he was much upset.

His immediate discomforture was occasioned by something else. On this day, the day Costello was missing, his pilots' flying log book had been placed in Dodd's cabin, by whom he knew not. A pilot did not part from his log book. His story told, a disconsolate medical officer left me to my thoughts. A trouble shared did not appear to have made him any more cheerful.

The ship was about the latitude of Gibraltar. After the wild weather of the preceding few days the sea was calm, the day sunny. Searches continued but nothing was found — no wreckage, no markers, nothing. A good pilot could ditch a Swordfish in a calm sea with some confidence and use his safety equipment. So went my thoughts. One of our aircraft was missing. Nothing was ever found. Why?

Was the aircraft the one we picked up without checking? Could it have been that the aircraft was widely off course? Were the compasses correct? I had no evidence to suppose that the aircraft was in anything other than perfect flying order, nor evidence to show that it was not. Was the observer overconfident and in error? Was he flying on a reciprocal bearing? What was Costello's frame of mind? He could be flamboyant and irrational. Who put Costello's log book in Dodd's cabin? Why?

I set down my recall of these events having made reference to my flying log for accuracy. They are sharply etched in my mind. Isolated and alone, I was fed with the evidence to think through the riddle of the missing aircraft and consider some

HMS *Nairana* and HMS *Activity* lying bow to stern at the mole Gibraltar, March 1944. This gives a clear impression on the limited space available for taking-off and landing and for manoeuvring aircraft on the flight deck. To compound matters, each ship had only one aircraft lift.

feasible solution. I have not been able to do so. I have not attempted to research some verifiable facts which could perhaps have led me to discount the faulty aircraft theory. Dismissing one possibility, other insoluble obscurities would still remain.

One of our aircraft was lost. It remains to me a haunting enigma.

Only a day or two after the loss of Dalton and Costello, there was a dramatic accident which led to a change in the squadron commanding officer and almost put an end to the squadron's operations altogether.

Our newly appointed CO, Lieutenant Commander Miller RN, was flying with Barringer as observer and PO Armstrong TAG. Returning after a patrol he made three or four attempts to land, but misjudged his approach every time. Unless the weather was exceptionally bad, which was not the case, an experienced pilot reckoned to get down quickly. The longer a carrier was committed to sail into wind to receive aircraft the more vulnerable she was. Miller's final effort was disaster. He hit the deck very heavily, tried to go round yet again, but hooked the top of the barrier. Only by coming down at full throttle on to the two Hurricanes parked forward of the barrier, thus seriously damaging all three aircraft, was the Swordfish and its crew saved from going into the sea over the ship's bow.

I was still recovering from my lumber pain. In this helpless situation it seemed that I was available as an 'agony aunt' for opinions and confessionals. Immediately he had, with difficulty, extracted himself from the stricken aircraft, Barry hastened, pale and shaken, to put a question to me. "How do you fuse depth charges, George?" It was not an academic question. He confided to me that, on inspection of the cockpit, it was found that the four depth charges the Swordfish was carrying were fused. I told him how the fuses were set by the pilot — only at such time as he was preparing to drop them in anger — not otherwise. Barry blanched, as did I, on realising how close we'd been to disaster. Over the bow and there would have been no Swordfish, Miller, Barringer or Armstrong and, quite possibly, no *Nairana*.

I was not privy to the enquiry which ensued. The upshot was that Miller was put under cabin arrest and Barry was ordered, as Senior Observer, to take over command of the squadron. That shook him, but he responded well to his new responsibilities. These, though onerous and unexpected, he must have felt were a better bet than by being piloted by the discredited CO.

We continued our patrols against submarine attacks and saw our sizeable convoy safely into the Clyde. It was all happening.

There was a short respite by the Tail of the Bank against our going out again. The trip had been so full of incident that I looked to arrange some holding hands with my fiance. We had no leave, but could forecast a day or two ahead. I got to a phone at Princess Pier, which mercifully worked after kicking it and rang Dorothy in a busy aircraft factory where she was engaged doing drawings for Lancaster bombers. She got my message after a few attempts and obtaining special leave — Yes, one had to be granted that to procure a forty eight hour pass from a wartime government factory — boarded a late train to Glasgow. I nearly lost her there, because Lt. Commander Bibby was also waiting to meet somebody and, seeing D, almost forgot who he was meeting! It was a brief romantic oasis, which restored some sanity to life, then I had to concentrate on things naval again.

Still off the Tail of the Bank, I determined to nip ashore. I scanned the duties board to confirm that I had none. I had. Officer of the Watch again. As I might have expected, it was the first watch, eight pm to midnight. Once more I was to be the one person responsible for the safety of the ship and its crew. This realisation could grow to a frightening degree if real or imagined threats arose. Alert a senior officer needlessly and get a rocket. Fail to do so in a dire emergency and God help him. Still, I was no longer a rookie.

We were anchored in the Clyde. It was winter, wet and very windy. Commander Healey was most shipshape, a neat and tidy person. On taking over the watch, I found that he had taken some preventative action. The gangway was his pride and joy. It was polished, painted and pomaded to perfection. It was precious. A hint of inclement weather and it was raised and stowed. It must not be exposed to any possibility of damage by any vessel coming alongside, so over the side went a scrambling net. All boarders must scramble.

The strong wind rose to gale force in gusts as night fell. Miscellaneous bits of flotsam floated past. A metal lighter, adrift from its moorings, narrowly missed the ship's side. The anchors held — no need to ask for assistance, or was there? No, I would risk it and pray all went well.

Then some action. Alongside came a drifter, returning liberty men from their carousal ashore. It pitched and rolled as skillful hands manoeuvred it. I peered over the side into the driving rain, concerned for the safety of those on the heaving slippery deck. Caps rammed on their heads, they jumped for the net, clung on and climbed the twenty feet to gain the boarding deck. Miraculously, so it seemed to me, none fell back on to the drifter, none into the sea. Inebriated sailors have a grip as vicelike as small infants or very old men.

I made the mistake of helping some tars over the ship's side. They were belligerent and showed no gratitude. Their intention was only to lay me out for my interference. A speedy retreat was necessary, some nifty footwork and the calling for reinforcements from their more sober pals to get the aggressive ones under control and below before they struck an officer, me, and were put on a charge. The excitement died down. The returnees reduced to a trickle. All were inboard. Stormy weather seemed like a calm after the insurgence. I made a final check to confirm all was clear. The last two heads appeared. The drifter pushed off and was away with despatch.

I turned to the deck to an astonishing sight. There stood Messrs. Timms and Gibbon, fitters and riggers to my aircraft, grand chaps, the salt of the earth. Although soaked through and singularly scruffy, they beamed with pleasure and displayed their prize — a size one Airedale dog! "Lift a heavy dog up a scrambling net?", you query. "It can't be done". It was. Little wonder the pair could keep my Swordfish airworthy.

I choose not to reveal the naval vocabulary I used. Their protestations about the morale boosting benefits of having a four legged friend fell on deaf ears. The saturated canine had board and lodging for the night and, presumably, was returned to shore as I decreed the following day. I saw it no more. So far as my watch was concerned, I had not seen it at all. It certainly didn't appear in the log.

I should not have been surprised at the ability of the pair, Bert Timms and Alf Gibbon, to acquire something the squadron needed, or that they thought it needed. The ubiquitous union of Stockport and Derby was formidable. They were amongst other things, enthusiastic soccer players. I played with them on squadron teams from

Flotta to Gibraltar. The opposition did not get past them easily.

One particular quirk they had was the compelling impulse to possess a dog. It became the squadron dog. It might be large or small, dog or bitch, thoroughbred or 'Heinz', black or white. The one constant thing about the dog 'in residence' was its name. It was always called 'Fred'. Saved complications I suppose. They had Fred everywhere when ashore, and seemed to have no difficulty in finding him or her, when changing stations, in a matter of hours.

February 24th saw us off to sea again escorting a convoy to Gibraltar. Things became exceedingly difficult in the hangar because we were lumbered with a sub flight of Fairey Fulmars with their crews, The Admiralty's conviction being that they would operate as night fighters. Regrettably the crews formed a separate little clique in the wardroom and behaved in a conceitedly superior manner. That manner completely collapsed one afternoon.

I did not regret it for I had reason to dislike them and, as nobody suffered any physical injury, there was no cause to weep. My dislike arose because, one evening, the Fulmar coterie were conversing rather too loudly in their preferred corner of the wardroom, when I overheard the name Alan Hodgson mentioned and dismissed with scorn as "that stupid bloody Swordfish pilot who killed himself". The reader will recall that Alan was my bosom pal, whom I greatly respected and had last seen when our ways parted after the completion of operational training. We had kept up a correspondence but there had been nothing from him for some time and I had heard, I know not how, that he had lost his life. Hearing my erstwhile friend spoken of so disparagingly, I lost my composure, rose from my chair and headed for the offender with evil intent. It was the only time during my service I can recall being really angry. My friend Alan I had personally known to be a splendid, salt of the earth, one might say noble character. My friends intervened and physically restrained me from achieving my objective.

As things stood, I was frustrated in being unable to satisfy my anxiety to know just what had happened to Alan, because I was earnestly counselled by my crew members to stay well clear of our Supernumerary aviators.

It took fifty years before I discovered what had occurred and that by corresponding with one of my old course members whom I contacted through the Fleet Air Arm Officers' Association.He had served in the same squadron as Alan in South Africa. Alan, being very keen to be 'up and at 'em', contrived a transfer to a Fulmar squadron on the same station as his Swordfish squadron, with active service on his mind. He was of the opinion that the transfer would enable him to achieve his end,because the Swordfish boys had not an immediate prospect of doing battle. He crashed, I understand, on his first flight in a Fulmar during an exercise — a simulated dog-fight. He was killed outright. He had received virtually no guidance on the flying characteristics of the Fulmar I understand. The aircraft was strange to him. A dog-fight on one's first flight in a strange aircraft! Little wonder that he stalled the aircraft in some manoeuvre.

Who, in charge, had been so remiss as to invite this tragedy? At least my question

The result of an attempt to make a night landing, March 1944.

had been answered. I was a sadder and wiser man, but somehow content in my knowledge of the facts

But, I must relate what happened.

The Swordfish had been doing all the work in reasonably heavy seas day and night. We'd had no evidence of enemy aircraft shadowing in the dark as far as we were aware. The hangar situation, with the one lift, was bad, because of the necessity to keep a Fulmar in a position so that it could be ranged quickly if required.

The weather improved. We were in calm sunny Atlantic seas at about latitude 36 degrees North. A request was made by the officer in charge of the Fulmar sub flight that they should be permitted to make a practice flight. The Captain consented. The aircraft was ranged and flew off. After a short period of flying around, it returned. The carrier turned into wind. The aircraft came in to land.

There was a fair gallery for those knowledgeable aviators. We were used to our squadron planes returning, but here was something different. Should things be difficult, or should the ship's crew be doubtful of a pilot's ability there were many who would come to watch. If there be a great conflagration ashore there will be spectators. Jack Teesdale and I stood together on the port bridge and watched. The pilot came in too low and did not correct, hit the roundown and the Fulmar's back was broken. The tailplane, rudder and part of the body was impaled on the stern. The wings and the rest of the aircraft veered to starboard, for which Jack and I were grateful and came to rest by the bridge angled over the side with one wing pointing skywards. As the ex Safety Equipment Officer, I applauded that the aircraft's dinghy inflated and remained in the middle of the deck. Nothing went on fire. The crew were virtually unhurt, except for their dignity. After a brief consultation with the maintenance experts, a decision was reached and the wreck was shoved over the side. There was more hangar space. The Captain was against Fulmars. Anything concerning them was shoved away forward away from the lift, far away!

Jack and I looked knowingly at each other and shared our thoughts. In our stores were two clocks, which, due to pressure of work, had not been fitted in the aircraft. They had been received in the stores after the aircraft had come aboard. Theoretically they were in the sea. It's an ill wind! It was a modest amount of flotsam for so much jetsam.

We continued our regular patrolling with a buoyant spirit. The weather returned to normal for the time of year which, in the Bay of Biscay, can be quite unpleasant. The clique in the wardroom had become mute. They had naught to do so far as I could detect. Flying with Dave Newbery, 'twixt midnight and morning, we got a contact and became excited until we discovered it to be an Eire merchant vessel. At least it was something to look at instead of featureless sea. I had mixed feelings about Eire considering where the country stood in the war — something like the look out post in Spain scanning Gibraltar.

We had a run of deck landing accidents as was to be expected. A Hurricane flipped on it's nose and picked up the arrester wires with it's prop, Al Burgham I think it was. A Swordfish flown by Lou Wilmot missed the wires one night and finished crashing into the barrier, as did the Hurricane. Night landings were more hazardous than day ones. There was much movement of the ship at times, especially if there was a lateral swell though the ship's head was into wind. It could produce a corkscrew effect by the stern. The pilot was not readily able to determine the angle of the deck at the precise moment of landing, yet it was essential that he land on the centre line at the right attitude to hook a wire at once on touching down. Because of the situations of aircraft in the hangar and the routine of servicing them, it was impossible to fly with any regularity in one's own aircraft — the one on which you had spent time trimming and perfecting — so far as one could perfect a Swordfish. I lost mine through mishaps by other pilots on more than one occasion and rescued my mascot panel from the damaged plane for transfer to another — until the novelty wore off.

Just in to March Lou Wilmot had another crash. Lou was the baby of the squadron. This was brought to our attention by the insistence on proper naval routine by Commander Healey. We were aboard on 31st December. It was the tradition that the youngest officer should perform the ritual of ringing sixteen bells to see the New Year in. Healey by diligent questioning, found that Lou was the man fitted for the job. He didn't want to do it, being of a retiring personality, pleasant and shy. With a show of embarrassment he rang the sixteen bells and the ship's crew welcomed in the New Year in the time honoured way. Lou retreated, glad to have got it over. Sadly it was Lou's last New Year.

In attempting to land at night he unfortunately got things wrong and, instead of remaining on the narrow deck, the Swordfish went over the starboard side of the ship and into the sea. Both Lou and his TAG, LA Ferguson, lost their lives. George Arber, his observer, was injured and much affected by the fumes from the smoke floats and flares which automatically ignited when the aircraft sank. George was kept in the sick bay, in a poor condition. His flying with 835 was over. I signed his report form in respect of 'Hurts and Wounds'. He is still in receipt of a pension for the damage sustained to his sight.

What followed was something we have not forgotten. Wilmot and Ferguson were buried at sea. It was a tragic and touching experience as, in the stillness of *Nairana*, her engines off, there remained only the sounds of the sea, the cruel sea. The bodies, shrouded by the Union flag, were slid over the side and committed to the deep, from whence they had been recovered, after a short but moving service. There was silence and a tear in many an eye.

It was then back to our duties.

Our work continued. We escorted a convoy back into the Clyde. We were glad to be back home for a breather. It was not to be. One of the Sea Lords, I know not which, flew over the Clyde, observed what he regarded as a clutch of carriers and questioned why so many were swinging at anchor off the Tail of the Bank. He obviously had some authority, because in forty eight hours we were off out again. Commander Healey, whose responsibility it was to reserve our berth, took note of what had happened. We had only just reached harbour. All of the other carriers had been in the Clyde much longer. He'd think about that.

The trip to Gibraltar was becoming a familiar one. Our protective flying saw both us and the convoys out and home safely. There were threats of enemy shadowing aircraft and of submarines, but nothing materialised because we had patrols airborne pretty well all the time. Some further accidents occurred on landing. Teddy Elliott had a barrier one. Eric McEwan went over the side — the second time that he'd crashed into the sea. Thankfully he was quickly rescued and soon recovered.

On returning we sailed up the Clyde but were surprised that we did not drop anchor in the usual place. Instead we crossed over to Helensburgh and berthed alongside. Commander Healey, as I have indicated, was a wily old fox. He reckoned we were not so open to prying eyes tucked in by the verdant foliage of the Scottish countryside. He was right. To our delight we got eight days leave. At this point the ship had a change of officer affecting us. our 'Wings', Edgar Bibby, who had been unwell, left and was replaced by Lt Cmdr Nigel Ball, RN. I got on very well with both officers and appreciated their friendly manner.

April saw us off again on convoy work. We seemed to be operating like a regular train service. Quite like a train service in that we delivered our passengers safely. The Gib' run was becoming familiar. I was getting used to the topography of the place. One place I found fascinating on the Rock was Rosea Bay. That was where Nelson was landed after his fatal wound at Trafalgar. There is a neat and well tended graveyard. The tombs of members of ship's companies by their inscriptions tell the

The author (left) with his Observer Sub Lt Thomas and Air Gunner Leading Airman De Fraine, HMS *Nairana*, 1943.

story of their privations on the seas and in conflicts. So many of them were but in their teens, So many of them perished from disease rather than in battles. Reading my way round this sacred plot I came to realise how well off we in *Nairana* were.

We were alongside rather than by the detached mole. There was no swinging at anchor or watchkeeping. A glance at the notice board — damn Sadler's on it again! This time it was 'Officer in charge of Church Parade'. It was a new duty and as usual I knew nothing of the routine. This was typical of the Navy. Constantly things were landed on you but you didn't know the drill. The thing to do was to search the ship for an experienced RN executive officer and ask him. I asked 'Torps' an RN Lieutenant, presuming that I saw our ship's company parade to church. I was wrong. 'Torps' said it was for all the ships in the harbour. I got ashore and lined up our lot.

Other officers came with their men, reported to me, saluted and scarpered! All of them. There seemed to be a flotilla in harbour. Somehow, single handed, I got them moving. I don't know if I lost any, because the main street to the cathedral is serpentine and I could not see the rear from my position at the head of the column. Approaching the imposing edifice I wondered how to bring the parade to a halt. Inspirationally I raised my voice to a screaming crescendo and roared "Break Step". CPO Willmott would not have approved, but it worked.

I let them find their own way back — just concentrated on my devotions.

Our return to the Clyde was busy but uneventful. We TBR pilots kept airborne and the subs remained submerged or so it seemed. We did some work in the Clyde including some night lighting checks. Opinion was expressed form sources outside the carrier, that our deck lighting was too bright and might therefore reveal or position to enemies when we were operating aircraft. Various experiments were made in an effort to meet the criticism,but of course pilots needed adequate illumination to effect safe landings. It was a tricky problem.

A dramatic accident caused us to put to sea again a couple of days late. George Gordon came in to land in his Sea Hurricane. The weather conditions were good and clear. For whatever reason, probably because his approach was too fast, when he cut his engine the aircraft did not ground, but floated and missed the arrester wires. Instead of maintaining course on the deck centre line he drifted to port.

Having nothing on and it being a pleasant day, there were about fifteen officers in the port catwalk opposite to the bridge. We were chatting and watching. I was one of them. As the Hurricane headed our way at speed, the danger was realised. The plane hit the barrier with considerable force with the engine just inboard of the stanchion which supported the port side of the barrier. Its port wing hung over the port side of the ship. The stanchion, being unaccustomed to this cavalier treatment, broke off at its base and was thrown into the air. It reminded one of a child playing 'piggy' with a tapered stick. It described a graceful parabola, then came down in the port catwalk with a crash. It hurt nobody, because there was nobody there. It demonstrates how quickly one can respond to a threat of imminent danger if pressed. The recent occupants of the catwalk, just below deck level, were in a disorderly heap — two companionways below! Talk about moving with alacrity.

George was out of the plane very quickly shaking like an aspen. He got away from his wrecked aircraft with haste and the flight deck fire crew were on the scene at once. Remarkably, although there was spillage of fuel, oil and coolant, there was no fire. George naturally needed some water of life to revive him and this was readily dispensed by other aircrew members, especially as he had gained us two more days to loaf about, partly ashore, whilst the stanchion was repaired. It was a substantial piece of equipment which one could not envisage being broken by an aircraft crashing into the barrier. A replacement was therefore not carried. Even our friends Messrs Timms and Gibbon had not got one!

By 12th May repairs were effected and we were to sea again. The stint ahead proved to be a hazardous one. Regardless of the month the Atlantic weather was bad. One did not spend any length of time on deck. The strong winds made it difficult to stand upright. Adaptions to *Nairana*'s flight deck lighting had been made. The outline lights were dimmed and hooded so that they could only be seen from astern and then but three degrees each side of the fore and aft line. Take off was risky. Outline lights were not allowed for take off. Only two vertical wands of light, about two feet six inches high were permitted. These were positioned port and starboard at the edge of the deck forward of the bridge. The pilot could not see them from a tail down position. He could not be sure that he was on the centre line until the aircraft tail was up. The deck width was sixty feet, the Swordfish's span forty six feet. It left little clearance from the bridge. A temporary solution was found. The four most experienced pilots would do the night flying. I had become of age and was one of four. It was not the perfect arrangement for several reasons, but we did it. After all, it was the month I was promoted to Lieutenant.

Chapter 11 — Walking on Water

The 21st May saw *Nairana* and Campania out on a hunting group. One carrier was to undertake routine patrols, the other was to stand by with strike aircraft. Stan Thomas, my observer and I, constituting a senior crew were allowed to see the tactical plot. As duty crew we had stood by all day without any call for flying and were ready to turn in. The weather was foul. Mountainous seas and gale force winds prevailed. We looked above deck and immediately came below again. There was absolutely no prospect of flying. The tactical plot showed no submarine contacts. We were about to retire to our shared cabin when Captain Taylor came into the Air Control Office.

He popped up onto the flight deck, then came down again. "Fine night to catch subs on the surface" he said. "Campania not flying? I'll fly". We listened and were prepared to join in the joke. Then we realised that he was serious. He meant it. Campania was the carrier on duty patrol. Her captain considered conditions unsuitable for flying. Captain Taylor, however, was the senior captain. He insisted "I'll fly". That did not mean him. It meant Tommy, our gunner de Fraine and me. We were severely shaken, but stood by whilst the Met officer Sub Lieutenant Mike Arrowsmith was summoned. We were horrified at the prospect of flying, but did not show our feelings. We stood by to obey orders.

Arrowsmith was eager to express his sentiments and did so to the Captain's great displeasure. He said that we were in an occluded front. He was quite unable to give wind speed or direction and he averred that flying in such conditions was not possible. As our intended patrol was to be by dead reckoning with radio silence, we wholeheartedly agreed, but did not voice our opinions.

A heated argument ensued between Sub Lieutenant and Captain. Poor

Arrowsmith, who had been called in to give advice, got a severe dressing down. Captain Taylor rejected all advice. We were to take off without delay. We dashed off to collect our gear to a desperate plea from Arrowsmith "For God's sake, try to find a wind as soon as you can".

Boarding the aircraft was difficult for both me and de Fraine but more especially for diminutive Tommy with his board and navigational gear. Getting airborne presented no difficulty — no need for concern about the centre line. We were off about one third along the deck. Following my normal practice I had set the altimeter at zero, which gave a tolerance of about forty six feet, the freeboard of the flight deck.

Our course was astern, downwind, so we were soon away from the carrier. We tried to find the wind strength and direction by use of a flame float. At one thousand feet, we could not see the float. We tried again at five hundred feet. The aircraft was so buffeted about that straight and level flight was impossible. Taking beam and quarter bearings was hopeless, the float not being visible because of the raging seas. We did the best we could in starting the designated patrol by Tommy's inspired guesswork our minds more concerned with our survival than upon submarines.

After about half an hour of steering rather speculative course, there was merciful relief. Somebody had second thoughts about our near impossible task. We received a radio signal to return to the ship.

Back into the gale we turned and Tommy operated the ASI. After what seemed too long a time as we clawed our way back, his relieved voice at last reported that

A poor quality newspaper photograph showing the HMS *Nairana* in heavy seas (at times the flight deck was at an angle of 45 degrees). This was the occasion when the author was ordered to take-off by Captain Taylor.

he thought we'd picked up *Nairana*. He gave a course to steer.

We got closer. At two miles away, Tommy's reassuring voice that we were now on the vertical screen. A slight correction and we were dead on course. Nearer we came, now only one mile ahead. I could see nothing. I came down to two hundred feet and peered ahead with eyes like organ stops, but still I saw nothing. Tommy indicated half a mile. Still no sign of anything. At a quarter of a mile, Tommy's attempted comforting voice had lost its conviction and became one of anxiety. He too peered ahead into the driving rain. Was the equipment faulty? Were we lost? Then we found the carrier. We were absolutely on course!

Although the altimeter registered two hundred feet, we cleared the ship's bridge about half a wingspan to port at an altitude just below the level of the flight deck. Having looked certain death in the face, I recovered from the shock and quickly adjusted the altimeter to zero and concentrated on landing. At least Tommy had found *Nairana*. He had done his part. It was now up to me.

The ship was into wind. Straightening up as best I could, I set the giro compass roughly in line with the deck lights and tried a landing circuit. The visibility was so bad that the carrier could not be seen at all on the downwind leg of my two hundred feet circuit. I had therefore to attempt a landing circuit purely on instrument flying. A two hundred feet circuit to land on an invisible aircraft carrier in vile weather on a pitch black night was a new and unwelcome experience.

Achieving a correct angle on a landing approach became more luck than judgement because of the very restrictive sighting arc of the deck lights. A dozen approaches into the storm and I could not get it right. Then — Almost disaster. Instead of approaching from the stern, I came in down wind over the bow, swinging to starboard just in time to avoid colliding with the bridge. Bill Cameron, the Deck control Officer, dived into his nets as we sped along the deck. The giro had precessed. Enough was enough for everybody. It was my last attempt to land that night. We were ordered to gain height and were vectored for over two hours until dawn broke.

Dawn breaking was not the best description of the next day. It brought no improvement to the weather conditions. Thankfully, though visibility was very poor, I could at least discern the carrier on a circuit. *Nairana* turned into wind. In the very heavy seas the carrier pitched fiercely. The roundown rose and fell considerably — at least thirty feet. Attempting to engage the first or second arrester wire in such conditions would be dangerous and most risky. I part sideslipped into a steeper than usual descent and picked up the third wire. Eager helping hands seized the aircraft. We breathed again. We were home and dry.

"Good show" said Captain Taylor. It was one of his favourite expressions if he was pleased. Tommy and I had the good sense not to express our feelings. We had been half a wing span from a watery grave and were mighty lucky to be alive. A letter from Stan Thomas written to me in 1984, shortly before he died, recalled the incident. It was etched indelibly on his mind. From his log he quoted "Visibility 50 yards, could not land on, stayed up till dawn, not a very nice experience!!! I think I was so shaken for days afterwards that I did not make as much fuss as I should have done". Stan was deeply religious, slow to wrath and never heard to swear, ever. Fuss or no fuss, the episode had a telling effect upon him. He was indeed shaken. On 29th May, only eight days later, during which time we experienced more excitement, if that be the most suitable way of describing our six nocturnal flights in a most unfriendly Atlantic Ocean, Tommy flew with me for the last time. It was his last flight with 835. He left for a shore appointment. I continued, thereafter piloting the CO, for a further five months.

As I reflect on our perilous petrol I am quite sure that the presence of my two crew members helped me. In the rear cockpit they could do nothing to aid our landing. They were not flying the aircraft. They were my responsibility. It was up to me to see they were safe. That they had confidence in me was all important. I found that my concern for them caused the fear for myself to be abated. I simply had a job to do and I got on with it.

The decision, entirely his own, by Captain RMT Taylor, that we should fly was a grave error of judgement. He risked three lives and an aircraft to no material advantage. It was the sort of thing that could happen when an aircraft carrier's captain, who lacked any real knowledge of flying requirements, insisted on deploying aircraft in the face of expert advice not to do so. The pressure on the Royal Navy to provide experienced seaman captains for the escort carriers resulted in officers from the retired list being recalled into active service. Small wonder that they were not versed in air warfare. On the other hand they should have been. Although trained as a pilot I was still meant to be an executive officer capable of taking my turn on watch. Should not the Admiralty have introduced some training and versatility into the working knowledge acquired by captains? I'd had enough trouble with a Commander's ignorance of parachutes.

Tommy and I did not retain an on going hate for our Captain, although we were greatly dismayed by his action at the time. His confidence in our ability was too optimistic for our liking even though his report on my flying prowess was most flattering and he regarded me as a good naval officer. Good job he didn't read my thoughts on the morning of 22nd May!

I mentioned DR, or dead reckoning navigation. In order not to advertise our presence to enemy ships or aircraft we often did our patrols without making radio contact with the aircraft carrier. The observer with his chart board on his knee in an open cockpit, illuminated at night by a small bulb clipped on about the intensity of a glow-worm, had to give his pilot courses to steer. These were determined by our finding the direction and strength of the wind which called for accurate flying. I heard a broadcast which researched into the loss of Major Glen Miller in the Norseman plane on a flight across the English Channel. The conclusion reached was that the Norseman was flying low over an area of sea which was used as a dropping point for bombs. Heavy bombers were sometimes unable to find their targets in

Germany because of adverse weather and did not drop their loads. Instead, they jettisoned their bombs in the designated area. In referring to the possibility that the Norseman was in the area when dropping took place, the spokesman said that it was within ten miles of it and "what was ten miles here or there". I did wish to ask him if he had considered the navigation of a carrier based plane on DR and with aircraft carrier and plane both changing directions. Ten miles could well be the difference between life and death. Finding land was easier than finding a floating base in an ocean.

There were many U-boat contacts and alarms from the too close company of reconnaissance aircraft. On 25th May, George Gordon and Sam Mearns were patrolling in their Hurricanes. The aircraft had been painted off white, which might make them sound easy too see. In the heavy clouded skies of the Atlantic they were difficult to spot. Too difficult for a U boat to spot. The fighter pilots saw the sub's periscope, which gave the indication that our convoy was about to be threatened. Unable to attack submarines with their armament, they called for TBR reinforcements. Johnny Hunt and I were at readiness and two Swordfish were ranged in haste. Johnny's was armed with depth charges, mine with armour piercing rockets.. I was convinced that we'd got the wrong weapons and, quite improperly I suppose, I approached Captain Taylor personally and requested that my aircraft be armed with 'Oscar', the acoustic torpedo. He said no. I implored him to accede to my request. Tommy recalled my having what amounted to a stand up argument with him over the matter. He would not relent and I flew off with rockets. My Swordfish was slow. The rockets were designed to attack submarines on the surface. By the time I reached the place where the submarine had been sighted, I saw only the wake left after it had submerged. The rockets were useless. An acoustic torpedo would have done the job perfectly and the sub's point of diving was sufficiently distant from the carrier for there to have been no danger of Oscar homing on *Nairana*. In any case, I would not have dropped the weapon in close proximity to the ship I was later to land on! Unfortunately, I could not convince our Captain and he was boss in all things. The thing was that I had done the original flying tests with the weapon. It was not conducive to comfortable flying because it weighed 850 lbs and was carried on a rack half way along the port wing. This made the aircraft unstable and caused the pilot to have the control column somewhere up his right armpit. Given permission to do as I desired, I would have achieved a kill without doubt. I was mightily frustrated. At least we put the sub off attacking the carrier, but we could have destroyed the menace.

Later two more Hurricanes flew off after a Ju 290 which got away before Al Burgham and Charles Richardson, who attacked it, could account for it. On their returning it was just beginning to get dark. Fighter pilots were not accustomed to and did not undertake night flying. Al came in too fast, possibly because the aircraft's flaps were not operating fully, missed the arrester wires and ploughed into the barrier. Although his gun button was set 'safe' a cannon shell remaining in the breech after his firing at the enemy aircraft was triggered by the impact and a shot struck the control tower. It just missed 'Wings', Nigel Ball, but he was wounded in the arm by splinters. Fortunately Richardson landed with out mishap. The injury sustained by Nigel Ball resulted in his going ashore on sick leave on our next return home.

The following day, the same pilots were off after another Ju 290 and, finding themselves in a favourable position above it, closed to attack from opposite quarters. They pressed their attack home, but Richardson's aircraft's wing touched the sea. The aircraft exploded. Al continued to attack the Ju 290 which also exploded and dropped into the sea. Al flew over looking for Charles but could see no survivors of either aircraft. A Swordfish search later found wreckage of both planes and one body which proved to be that of Charles Richardson. His body was picked out of the sea by the escort vessel Highlander.

Later in the day Mearns and Wallis, in their Hurricanes, were sent to intercept approaching enemy aircraft. Again they proved to be Ju 290s, two of them. One of them they shot down into the sea. The other escaped into cloud cover. In this instance there were some German aircrew survivors who were later picked up by one of our escort vessels.

The sadness of another burial at sea took place the following day when Richardson was given the same ritual as Lou Wilmott. Highlander came alongside the carrier so that proper respect could be given by the carrier's crew to one of its much loved members. The service, brief but solemn, with flags at half mast, silence, engines off is a most reverent and touching experience.

May '44 had been a month of feverish activity and vile weather. There were many attempts by our enemies to attack us and we had done a great deal of flying. The fighters had concrete evidence of their successes and indeed of their sad loss. The Swordfish had nothing concrete but the satisfaction that their constant patrols resulted in our having no loss of shipping, either RN or merchant. There was therefore the feeling of a job well done at the end of each day. With the senior crews, such as Tommy and I, it was hard to detect when a days work was done with our being night aces.

Along with all this pressure I detected a touch of levity. It was essential, so I thought, that one should retain a sense of humour.

The Deck Landing Control Officer's job was onerous. Being on the exposed deck day and night when aircraft were landing was hard graft. Bill Cameron was tired as were we all. It was a satisfied tiredness because, though we'd had a busy flying day with many enemy threats, we'd come through it well. Following dinner, the officers retired to the wardroom. Around the electric fire secured to a bulkhead was a fender seat and Cameron had claimed a comfortable warm position perched upon it. Replete after dining well, he, without warning, broke wind so precipitately that the wardroom reverberated. I assert that the ship's crest swung and the brassware rattled! It certainly shook Commander Healey. "Stop that Cameron" he roared.

Without any hint of a change of expression on his heavy tired visage, Cameron replied "Yes Sir. Which way did it go?"

Below decks there was also the satisfaction of a job well done. It was more tiring to be on lookout, whether one be aboard ship or on a long aircraft patrol, than to be doing something which demanded physical effort or quick thinking. The eyes glazed over scanning the featureless sea. On the same day as Cameron's fabulous fart, a member of the deck handling crew was delighted to have been involved with the many sorties flown. It was all go and there was a real sense of purpose about the ship's activities. Taffy addressed me. Proudly he said in his strong South Wales accent "Did you see me Sir, dashing about on the flight deck like a blue arsed fly as it were?"

I'd not heard it put quite like that before, but I knew exactly what he meant.

Having experienced severe storms at sea, we were in harbour at Gib' with the aircraft carrier *Campania*, our sister ship. We ribbed their aircrews about the behaviour of their vessel in heavy seas. It pitched. It rolled. It took seas over its bow and generally behaved like a coracle in a waterfall. We were met with derision and advised that *Nairana* was worse. To prove their point they produced a photograph of *Nairana* during a particularly rough period of our turbulent passage and we had to admit that they had got a point. It rather shook me to have pictorial evidence of the conditions under which we Swordfish torpedo bomber reconnaissance crews were flying — a case for the bard "O wad some Pow'r the giftie gie us to see oursels as others see us!" Mind you, we felt to some degree proud about it and maybe there was some apprehension.

The ship's movement did not suit all on board. Some were seasick and did not easily overcome it. I found that if one kept occupied with something it helped. One morning during breakfast the ship changed course about ninety degrees and the pitching motion became a rolling one because of a huge swell on the beam. The mess tables were athwartships and the lazy stewards had neglected to fit the mess traps, which prevented crockery from sliding off the tables, so that much of it was broken. The Commander occasionally permitted us to set up a table tennis table in a space in the mess when it was clear. To witness play on a rolling deck was hilarious, because the players were unable to keep their feet. Anticipating the ship's movement and planning a return to take advantage of it was very difficult. Moving about the ship one had to take care to avoid injury. One had to tread warily, particularly on open deck areas, not rush and get ones 'sea legs'. It was easy to miss ones footing on a companionway, to crash into an unyielding bollard on a wet deck. The answer was that we got used to it and took care. There were accidents but they were relatively few, because it took but a short time for us to learn. There is a difference between what I call an accident and carelessness, which is often an accident waiting to happen — rather like the art of Laurel and Hardy.

Early June we were escorting another convoy to Gibraltar. It proved to be less hazardous than the preceding trip, for which I was grateful. Performing heroics with my heart in my mouth kept the circulation in good shape, but I was quite content to settle for the landsman's cry for a "fair and gentle breeze" without any alarms. We enjoyed our cruise to the Med' and back. Stan Thomas had left the squadron before we sailed, so I was piloting Barringer, the CO. Over two years I had progressed from being a new boy to being effectively Senior Pilot. We did our usual Swordfish patrols and the enemy didn't give us much trouble.

Whilst in Gib' we had some time ashore and my name didn't feature much on the Duty Officer list. *Nairana* was by the detached mole which was inconvenient, because I could not just nip a shore for an evening stroll one very humid day. I needed water transport. Peering over the rail, I saw a boat alongside. Confirming from the coxswain that it was going ashore, I nipped over the side and waited. A couple of minutes later Captain Taylor arrived. The boat's crew came smartly to attention and so did I. "Hello Sadler where are you going?" the Captain enquired. Embarrassed by being discovered in his boat, I explained apologetically that I had intended going for a walk. "No you're not" he said. "You're coming with me to see the Flag Officer". I found myself checking the smartness or otherwise of my number two uniform.

It proved to be a most pleasant evening. The Captain and I had a continuous interesting conversation as we climbed the Rock. Eventually we reached the Flag Officer's eyrie. His residence, 'The Mount', set high on the Rock with spectacular views across to North Africa, was surrounded by four acres of grounds purchased by the Navy Board in 1799. This imposing edifice was used for many years as 'home' for Flag Officers, Gibraltar. The Staff Officer appeared and reported our arrival. The Captain meanwhile saw that I wrote my name in the visitors book. I wondered what would happen next.

The Flag Officer came in. I was introduced, then he and the Captain retired to an inner room. I then discovered what a Staff Officer did. He led me aside where he plied me with pink gins and pleasant conversation against the time the senior officers had finished their chat. Captain Taylor had known the Flag Officer for some years. They were old friends.

We lower orders aboard *Nairana* were disrespectful to the Flag Officer, Gibraltar. His abbreviated title, 'FOG', amused us and we unkindly thought of him as a muddle headed senior officer like a character in the radio comedy *The Navy Lark*. The 'fog' lifted as soon as I was introduced, I thought of him thereafter with respect and also with sympathy. Who'd want to be stuck on the Rock? Who'd want the responsibility of being in charge of it?

My evening walk was a most rewarding experience. A Captain who was generous enough to invite my company and take me up to the Headquarters obviously had soon regard for me. His order to me on this evening proved to be so different from the one received to get airborne in vile conditions but a month before. It seemed that I had gained his respect. I appreciated that.

It was pleasant at Gibraltar in the summer out of the cold miserable North

Atlantic. We got a gallery of 835 Squadron officers at the bull fights at La Linea and Algeciras occasionally, but the bullfight novelty had largely worn off and most of us disliked the spectacle. Sometimes, if off duty, the officers were permitted to walk through the honeycomb of the Rock and emerge into Sandy Bay for a dip.

One morning, I managed an unauthorised escape to join other officers for a bathe. Included in our little group, only five or six of us, was the Torpedo Officer, an RN Lieutenant. His name escapes me probably because we habitually called him 'Torps'. He was pleasant enough, but laughed little and generally wore an unsmiling visage. To compensate, he had a dry sense of humour. He could also be very funny quite unwittingly, when he was being serious. We reached the bay and disported ourselves in the sun. We were the only people on the sizeable beach.

Before long, two Gibraltees, obviously man and wife, came on to the beach with a young infant They ran into the water holding the child by the hands about two hundred yards from us. The child cried out in exuberance.

Torps looked along the beach with a hurt expression. "It's getting like bloody Margate" he pronounced.

I found there was an engineer officer, Sub Lt Evans, on board who lived in my home town and with whom I had common acquaintance. He was most interested in our armour piercing rocket projectiles and their performance. I told him about them, enthusing over what I rated as a superb weapon when used on the proper target. My assurances, I could see did not convince him. He was obviously sceptical. Given permission to do some firing, I took him up with me on the Mediterranean side of the Rock. I dropped a smoke float, flew away some distance then returned and made a mock attack. He was amazed at the smoothness of their launching, the speed of delivery and the accuracy as my salvo of rockets splattered the sea beside the float.

It was a great surprise to him as it must have been to some U-boat commanders that a Swordfish, the slowest of our carrier aircraft, could deliver so devastating an attack from long range with such velocity and precision. It could perhaps be compared to a chameleon, standing so motionless that it might be taken for an ornament, uncoiling its tongue like lightning to catch a fly. At least brother Evans was impressed.

On our return trip Barry and I found a quiet moment — no flying. We leant on the rail by the stern of *Nairana*. In a reflective mood Barry produced some coins of small denomination and pitched them one at a time into the sea. He bid me observe the little hands rise above the waves and take them. It was a magical distraction. Little did he realise that he was following an old Celtic practice. About 2000 BC, a tribe, having captured some of their foes, beheaded them and threw the heads into a river where they were washed downstream. The decapitated bodies were buried elsewhere. This barbaric procedure they believed would ensure victory over their enemies. It was not Barry alone who perpetuated this. Take a park or ornamental garden with a pool and observe public behaviour. People will toss coins, with heads on them, into the water. Why? They do so for good luck. There were times when we needed good luck so, following Barry's lead, I joined in. Mythology? Maybe. We both survived.

Chapter 12 — All Change

Back home again we disembarked ashore to HMS *Ringtail*, an air station in Lancashire close to Southport. Here the TBR side of the squadron was re-equipped. It was not with a new sleek streamlined aircraft, but with the Swordfish Mark III. This new version of our familiar friend had even more gear heaped upon it. The Mark III very obviously had something different because if ever an aircraft looked pregnant the Mark III did. Housed in a massive dome under the belly of the fuselage between the undercarriage wheels, was the new ASVX. This transmitter receiver scanner was the last word. It could detect U-boats at a greater range than the earlier ASV whilst U-boats could not so easily pick up the aircraft's transmission. From the pilot's point of view there was a reduction in performance. The Swordfish was in no way streamlined but the 'belly' really settled things. It resulted in a lower maximum speed, a higher stalling speed and it took a greater wind speed, a longer run or the assistance of rockets to get airborne. The rear cockpit was revolutionised. Sophisticated equipment took up what had been the observer's cockpit. The observer had to move aft and, like musical chairs, the rear gunner was out. After our close relationship with our three man crews, it was a sad loss. I felt sorry for them. There was no avenue of escape for them, because few Fleet Air Arm planes called for Telegraphist Air Gunners. They found themselves out of a flying job and were assigned to other duties.

Both pilot and observer were now in very cramped conditions. Controls for the weapons were difficult for the pilot to reach, because he was strapped into the cockpit. A favourite position for switches was behind ones shoulder blade. Also, facilities were such that one had to remain continent for the duration of a patrol. The observer in the rear ex-TAGs smaller and more exposed cockpit, faced forward to operate the ASVX and backward to attend navigational and radio duties. It would have been small wonder had the observers incurred serious spinal damage. Maybe some of them did. As usual we adapted to the new way of life, no doubt grumbling sotto voce. There was better equipment indeed, but the vehicle for transporting it was groaning under the strain.

After a little leave from which I returned early so that Barry and I could test out our new equipment, we experimented along the Lancashire coastline. I was most impressed that, flying just off the shoreline along Blackpool promenade, Barry was able to pick up all three of Blackpool's piers with absolute accuracy on the ASVX — with the tide out at that! I glanced over my shoulder to check that he wasn't cheating and looking over the side, but he wasn't. Our pleasure over the efficiency of the set and Barry's quickly acquired skill at operating it, caused us to forget about other aircraft. I understand that complaint was made from Squires Gate airfield at Blackpool about an aircraft flying against regulations over their flight path. Fortunately they knew not from whence it came nor where it went and we took pains not to advertise our flight. I did not see or interfere with any other aircraft, but apparently we flew at right angles to and just west of their runway. We hardly knew it was there being so occupied with our test. I couldn't resist a bit of mischief. Lytham St Annes had an open air swimming pool with a high diving board. A youth was poised on its top, with the air of an Adonis attracting attention before he performed his dive. Accustomed to low flying, I was much lower than was officially permitted and he was directly in my sights as I turned for Burscough. His graceful contortions were abruptly terminated as our pregnant plane bore down on him at eye level and, though doing no serious damage to himself, his entry into the pool no doubt fell short of his intentions. The front view of a Swordfish would alarm anybody.

Having familiarised ourselves with the performance of our new plane and its equipment, I repaired with other Swordfish pilots to nearby Inskip for some brief training with Rocket Assisted Take Off. It took little learning. The technique was to advance the throttle as in a normal take off, gain speed so as to be in a tail up posture. When approaching the correct speed for take off the aircraft was returned to a tail down attitude and the rockets were fired. These, one on each side of the lower mainplane angled slightly outwards and downwards gave impetus to lift the plane into the air. Once airborne the rocket canisters were jettisoned at some suitable place by activating a lever — just some more in the way of controls — the rocket firing button and the jettison lever!

That sorted, I found that the squadron was due for further changes, this time in personnel.

The changes started at the top. Captain Taylor left and was replaced as captain of *Nairana* by Captain Villiers Nicholas Surtees, DSO, RN. He looked in at Burscough to see his squadron. Regrettably he was not in anywise a flying officer, his previous career, where no doubt he had served with distinction, being in cruisers. Out of retirement to take command of an aircraft carrier without any experience of the techniques and limitations of flying from one, might be regarded as unwise, but the ways of the Admiralty were sometimes inscrutable. Possibly some land based drafting officer was detailed to insert square pegs into round holes the which he did with admirable precision.

Lt Cdr Nigel Ball, our Commander Flying, returned from sick leave, his damaged arm mended. I felt that he was going to be busy if he was intending to proffer aeronautical advice to our new and zealous captain. The Captain very obviously had a mind of his own.

The change affecting me personally was that Barringer, The CO, having regard to his long service in both the Mediterranean and the Atlantic, had a discussion about his future with Nigel Ball. The upshot was that he was recommended to take a shore appointment the which he did. This resulted in our having a new Commanding

Officer. Again it was an observer CO, Lt Cmdr Val Jones, RNVR, ex 811 Squadron, which had flown from HMS *Vindex*, a British built carrier similar to *Nairana*. From Val's arrival until I left the squadron I was his pilot. Jack Teesdale, a senior observer and our Stores Officer left the squadron, so I took over as Stores Officer. "All change," sounds like the call of a conductor at a transport terminus. To me it meant a new plane, a new observer and a new job. From his arrival I got on exceedingly well with Val Jones. On our patrols it was as though we had crewed together for a considerable time. We trusted each other implicitly which, out over a wide expanse of ocean, often in most inclement weather, was essential to our welfare. We took things philosophically and did not flap.

As it happened, I had an early opportunity when piloting Val Jones to exercise my judgement to good effect. It was on my first flight with him from *Nairana*. I had flown Barringer, the retiring CO aboard and was now flying the new CO off. The trip was but five minutes duration, the least one could record in a log book, we went to the nearest five minutes, because it was only to demonstrate the use of Rocket Assisted Take Off. The aircraft being light, that is unloaded, I was able to remain airborne at the absolute minimum speed above stalling. I aimed to do the gentlest landing ever. Out to impress I was. I approached in copybook manner, was actually over the stern and on the point of cutting the throttle, when 'Bats' waved me round. The situation was one where it is absolutely essential that the pilot assesses the position instantly and acts on his own judgement. To have attempted to open up and go round again on another circuit from the speed to which the Swordfish was reduced and its angle of attack, would certainly resulted in the hook catching in the top of the barrier, if not flying directly into it. That would have meant disaster. Lt

The author's 178th deck landing, HMS *Nairana*, 14 August 1944. Note the ASVX radar housing and the rocket racks on the aircraft.

Commander Miller did just that, damaging three aircraft and his reputation.

Disregarding 'Bats' frantic waving, I put the Swordfish down. Although the landing was perfection I did not pick up a wire and stop as I had anticipated. Realising that something was amiss, I braked. The aircraft tail rose high. I eased the brake off, then braked again and proceeded down the centre line of the deck in a jerky kangaroo fashion, no doubt shaking up Val's digestive organs. It was important that I kept the aircraft straight, not the easiest thing with Swordfish brakes. Our forward progress reduced and the plane went up to the barrier and gently touched it. There was no damage to the aircraft excepting for a burst rear tyre.

The reason for my being waved round, was because the aircraft's arrester hook was not down. For some reason, the lever I had activated for my lowering it had not operated properly. Unfortunately, the Deck Control Officer did not give me the correct signal, a rotating paddle movement with his bats, which would have advised me of the fault and would have given me the opportunity to have another go at the erring release lever. He had so little cause to use the signal, because the situation was a very uncommon one — unique in my experience, that perhaps it didn't come readily to mind.

Fortunately no harm was done, excepting for the burst tyre and my great irritation. It was the first time that I had even touched the barrier and this was my 178th landing on carriers. It was far and away the best record in the squadron and the most deck landings. My own aircraft had been damaged on a few occasions by other pilots. One of the crashes was a complete write off.

Val was more than satisfied that I could land on without an arrester hook and said so. For my part I was chagrined that there should be any sort of mishap on our very first carrier flight. Val sympathised. Our camaraderie was forged from the outset.

Making sure that our aircraft were ready for operations kept us busy. I returned from Maydown, in Northern Ireland, leading six Swordfish aircraft. With two observers to check the bearings and make the necessary adjustments and ground crews to manhandle the aircraft on to the compass base, we got the job done. It was essential that there be no errors in that quarter. I was prepared to relax when the CO made a request. Lt Burgham, the leader of our fighter wing, said he was desperately in need of some spare parts for some of his planes. Indenting for them had proved fruitless. Val Jones asked me to put some overnight gear in a bag and fly over to Perth, where the stores warehouse was located and try to get some. I quickly put some things together, had some refreshment and was ready.

Having received the six Swordfish, *Nairana* had anchored in Rothesay harbour. I flew off with the aid of Rocket Assisted Take Off and, using pilot navigation, enjoyed a delightful trip on a summer evening to Scone, which I judged to be the nearest convenient airfield to Perth. It had been a glorious day. I could scent the pine trees in my open cockpit. I landed at Scone, which was a most attractive small airfield, where I found a number of RAF Officers with Tiger Moth aircraft. They were intensely interested in the Swordfish, which compared in a way with their craft its being a biplane apart, that is, from its curious underbelly. The 'belly', our ASVX, was meant to be new and secret and certainly not subject to anybody's inspection. There was no hangar where it could be secured overnight, so I had to take off again and fly to the naval air station at Errol, which proved spartan in the extreme.

The following day, a vehicle with a Wren driver was made available and we drove to the stores at Perth. I searched the storage racks in the warehouse and personally picked out the stores we urgently needed. They were in stock, all of them, but the squadron's requests appeared to have been disregarded. I was mightily annoyed that essential spares, the lack of which could prevent our fighter aircraft from operating, had not been sent to us. I expressed my sentiments freely. My impression of the competence of the Stores Staff was pretty poor. They were left in no doubt of what I thought.

Opinions ventilated, I was on my way back with the goods. The return was to me an interesting and new experience. The carrier was still at anchor in Rothesay harbour. The windspeed was rated at nineteen knots. A manoeuvre into wind by the carrier, still at anchor and I landed on. It was the only time that I took off from and landed back on an aircraft carrier in harbour.

The shortcomings of the Naval Stores had its flip side for me. I had the novelty of making a harbour to harbour flight in a fixed wing aircraft. It was a unique squadron experience. It never happened again. It was also satisfying because I had managed to locate the stores, obtained the requirements to keep the fighters airborne and in effect was both the indenting and delivery officer. It was much like the present DIY arrangement. As it happened, the items were obtained at the eleventh hour, because the following day we were at sea on convoy duty and that night I was on my first patrol with Val. Where to? We were bound for Gibraltar.

No sooner did we put to sea than the weather deteriorated. Val Jones and I did the longish night patrols. The CO was always at the forefront of things, especially if the conditions were bad. There were some scares of possible shadowing from German aircraft, but the weather was unsuitable for the fighters to fly and no submarine attacks resulted from the suspected enemy reconnaissance aircraft activities. One might say that the trip was uneventful. It was strange that even in the summer the Bay of Biscay could be so wild and inhospitable, though Gibraltar was calm and hot.

Our new commanders had settled in. They proved to be quite different in personality. Surtees, the Captain, desired action and attack unremittingly. As it happened we found neither submarines nor aircraft to attack either going out or returning, although on our homeward trip we sailed close in to the Portuguese coast 'trailing our tails' to entice German ships which were thought to be there. No action was joined and Surtees became restive. Val Jones, our Commanding Officer, on the other hand was more a thinking man, thinking in respect of the safety and welfare of his squadron members. He also knew something about the weather conditions in which an aircraft could reasonably fly. Surtees didn't. With the change of aircrews, we had some rather inexperienced pilots and observers who were worthy of consideration in inclement weather. What was acceptable as opposed to hazardous did not concern our Captain overmuch. We escorted convoys to the Rock and back once more without any losses. We were doing our job satisfactorily or so we thought.

I felt sorry for a handsome young Sub Lieutenant, not one of our flying officers, on duty as Officer of the Watch at Gibraltar. The ship was at anchor, the gangway down on the starboard side and Captain Surtees was coming off shore in a dinghy. He was a harsh demanding man. One thing he had strongly criticised was the most unsatisfactory manner in which he was piped aboard. This had resulted in some practising by the bo'sun to get things exactly right. It was a bright sunny day and the Subbie was in Number 5s, his white uniform, looking immaculate. The dinghy passed ahead of *Nairana*, down her port side and round her stern to come alongside the gangway. The carrier, like all escort carriers, had no quarterdeck. The only way to gauge the progress of the dinghy was to go through the passageway midships from starboard to port and judge exactly when to bring the reception committee to attention, station the bo'sun and do the piping. Our smart Subbie was on edge. He passed through the waist of the ship, waited to observe the boat reach the stern and returned at a rate of knots to alert his men. Unfortunately he unexpectedly met somebody on his return journey and was unable to avoid a violent collision. The 'somebody' was a rating returning from the galley to the mess bearing a dixie of thick pea soup. He was unable to deliver his messmates their first course. It was decanted over the OOW from his chest down to his shoes. I can recall his sad expression as he stood rigidly to attention saluting, whilst the bo'sun trilled on his pipe to perfection.

I happened to be nearby at the time, but melted into oblivion directly Surtees addressed his junior officer. The Captain's face expressed fury in scarlet. His utterance expressed his sentiments lustily, but then he had no sense of humour. If he had, I neglected to observe it. He gave no credit at all for his reception. The piping was absolutely spot on.

Early September saw us back in the Clyde and there were more changes. The fighter section was re-equipped with Grumman Martlet Wildcats so there was need for a short familiarisation course for the pilots at Yeovilton. The new aircraft had their pros and cons. The performance was superior to the Sea Hurricanes, the wings folded so that they were more manoeuvrable and they could be more easily stored in the hangar. There was perhaps less stability on landing, because the undercarriage was narrower than the Hurricane's. At least the Wildcat was designed for carrier flying whereas the Sea Hurricane was essentially a land based plane adapted for carrier flying.

One might have thought that, having done all the work, we TBR crews might be able to relax whilst the fighter boys learned about their Wildcats, but not a bit of it. Surtees determined that we would profit from training as though we'd not been doing the real thing without the opportunity to get rusty. We exercised in the Clyde practising new kinds of attack, firing flares beyond dummy targets at night then following up with a rocket attack amongst other new ideas. Val Jones, the CO, was not in empathy with Surtees. The two were not on the same wavelength. There was not the desirable bond between them to get on with our duties with an harmonious bonhomie and it showed.

Val thought it a good idea for us to fly ashore to Machrihanish for a day or two and submitted to the Captain that we should do so in order to do some night flying. Surtees smelt a rat and responded that the intended purpose of our going there was to renew our acquaintance with the Wrens and enjoy some leisure activities. One might fairly regard Surtees as a misogynist. He made the allegation with some spirit. Val assured him that was not the case, though I must admit that it had crossed our minds. Surtees reluctantly relented. We flew off to Machrihanish. Val had a night flying programme arranged immediately, and we did some flying on the day of our arrival ashore. Having finished flying, sometime just short of five o'clock in the morning, Val sent a personal signal to the Captain advising him of the number of pilots who had done night exercises that night. I mind his satanic smile as he commented that his message "would disturb the bugger's sleep". It did. So did the two commanding officers, of ship and squadron, rub along together.

Flying at sea was doing something useful and constructive. Exercising from naval air establishments was of course necessary, but boring and tedious. A bit of flying for fun was rare but enjoyable. An incident in this vein occurred in Machrihanish. One day the wind was full gale. There was no prospect of running any flying programme. We were restless. Hanging around the Squadron Office was dismal. Val Jones recalled that a friend of his in the RAF was stationed at Port Ellen. He was in Air Control. Val suggested that we two fly over to see him. Having a spot of lunch away from Machrihanish appealed, as did flying in exhilaratingly adverse conditions. I was delighted. We saddled a Swordfish and took off. It was a flog. The Swordfish was not a swift steed and flying pretty well into wind reduced our ground speed to what seemed walking pace, except that we were flying over the water.

We got to Port Ellen, a windswept airfield with no sign of aircraft except for a cocooned Anson tethered close to the Control Tower, alighted and met up with Val's friend, an RAF Flying Officer. He was as hospitable as he could be, but the 'lunch' was somewhat unbalanced. The trip was arranged on the instant and the mess, being rudimentary, was unprepared for visitors especially unexpected ones. There was virtually no food excepting for potato crisps. Both Val and I were great trenchermen and we were 'fair clemmed', to use a Northern expression.

The liquid refreshment side presented no difficulty. I know not which distillery provided the spirit. I do know that Islay boasted the single malts Lagavulin, Laphroaig, Ardbeg, Bowmore, Bruichladdich, Bunnahabhain, Caol Ila and Port Ellen. Although mindful of the fact that I was driving, consequently restricting my consumption of the "water of life" to something below Val's, I partook of a liberal libation. The sociable chatting done, we had to return to the Mull of Kintyre.

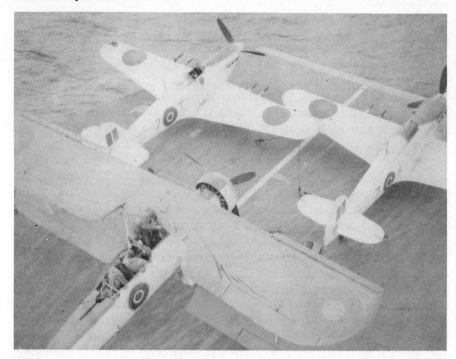

A Swordfish (showing clearly the seating positions of the pilot, observer and air gunner) and two Sea Hurricanes.

Fortified against the noisy elements, we stepped out of the Air Watch Office and on to the perimeter track. With single minded purpose, I surveyed the airfield and its common triangle of runways. I determined that they were all unsuitable for take off. I intended to face directly into wind, which was still blowing at gale force. My eye fell upon a very short stretch of perimeter track about a plane's width which looked right. I announced my intention of getting airborne from it instead of from the duty runway, unless our friend, the Air Watch Officer, could turn that runway into wind. He couldn't do so. I resolved to follow my plan.

Immediately the air was filled with vehement protests that I should on no account proceed as I intended. The AWO implored me not to do so. He appealed to Val to prevent me. Val would have none of it. His confidence in his senior pilot's judgement was uncrushable. "If George says he can do it, he can do it", asserted Val, brushing his friend's protests aside. Disregarding the AWO's frenzied signals and his clinging to the wingtip, I lined up the plane, warmed up with the brakes firmly on, pushed the throttle to override and trundled off. We had made little progress when I saw something I had not noticed before. Across the track were some overhead wires, telegraph, I think. A sudden heaving on the stick, a providential mighty gust of wind and the faithful Swordfish responded like a show jumper. Over the wires we went.

We had to descend almost at once to regain airspeed then we were up and away.

In the strength of the inner spirit I had triumphed over wind and wires. It was a heady experience.

Val's Flying Officer friend had to return to his Air Watch Office which was down wind from where we had become airborne. What about a beat up? Val agreed. I had the poor AWO prostrate thrice before he scrambled into his office. On reflection it was a scurvy trick to play on mine host, but he took it in good part and no doubt his uniform recovered after a good brushing. He probably thought that a Swordfish was quite a fast plane, flying with a full gale astern.

Our return to Machrihanish was quite majestic. It took only half the time of our outward flight according to my log book.

Chapter 13 — A Chilling Experience

Our brief spell at Machrihanish over, we were back aboard *Nairana* perfecting our skills. To my dismay, I had my one and only crash on my 199th deck landing. Val Jones and I were up on a night exercise, a glowworm illuminated cartridge attack, on a towed target in the Clyde. It was very dark. There was virtually no wind and I was unhappy with the aircraft's performance. It was sluggish and heavy. It was a 'Blackfish', as we pilots called the Blackburn manufactured Swordfish, which were not favourites with us. The towing vessel did not appear. We searched for it to no avail. I could hardly blame the local seamen for not turning up. It was a hazardous business towing a target not too far astern, to be attacked by an invisible aircraft out of a pitch black night.

The attack was aborted and we returned to the carrier. The aircraft behaved unsatisfactory, the engine not responding to the throttle settings. Because of the windless conditions, I requested, through Val, that I might jettison my weapons to reduce weight before landing on. My request was refused. On my approach the plane was slightly low and did not respond as I opened the throttle to increase power. The hook caught the roundown and was rammed up into the fuselage. Safety was the watchword. Straight up the centre line and into the barrier we went as the surge of power came too late. Val and I were unhurt. I had learned from observation that one must remain on the deck above all else. Pity I didn't make my 200th deck landing without accident, but I did achieve by far the best deck landing record in the squadron. I was never the less most displeased.

There was opportunity for me to use all my expertise on our next adventure. We put to sea and sailed for Scapa Flow. Rumours confirmed, we were to escort a convoy to Murmansk. This convoy was different from the others we had escorted. There were thirty merchant vessels, many escort warships and no less than three escort carriers, *Nairana*, *Vindex* and *Tracker*. Vice Admiral Dalrymple-Hamilton flew his flag in *Vindex*. Round the clock air patrols were planned for the TBR planes, eight hours on, sixteen hours off. It was intended that this convoy get through without loss — a challenge to the U-boats. There was also to be a greater challenge to air crews — the weather.

From the time we joined the convoy conditions were atrocious. High winds and mountainous seas raged. Visibility was bad. The convoy vessels were so tossed about that I could not comprehend how the smaller escort ships managed to keep station. They appeared and disappeared from view as the massive waves swept remorselessly across the foaming seas. On the carriers we found things unstable because, beam on, they rolled to something between 35 degrees and 40 degrees and caused us at times to wonder wether they would right themselves. They did and we ploughed on North.

Nairana was quickly on duty and Val Jones and I were first off to sample the conditions. Into wind the carrier pitched madly. The dawn patrol, which we did in these Northern waters, was in effect night flying because the hours of daylight were few. It was cold and uncomfortable but we did our patrols satisfactorily without untoward incident, finding nothing upon which to drop our depth charges. Landing was a bit tricky, but we put down safely. That done, other crews followed.

Our next duty stint on 27 October we were further North and it was noticeably colder. Conditions were hazardous for flying, but reports implied that there were many U-boats about. It was therefore desirable that an air patrol be maintained ahead of the convoy. We were now in a corridor between pack ice and the Norwegian Coast. *Nairana* on duty, Surtees in charge and Val and I were in the first Swordfish to get airborne, McEwan and Eames, Unwin and Legood followed. Just to add to what I was to carry was a revolver. Whoever reckoned that I should take it , incase I found myself crash-landing in Norway, wanted me to wear a holster! It was bad enough in the pilot's open cockpit in the freezing weather, wearing an Irvine Jacket, parachute, inner and outer gauntlet gloves and escape boots, hardly able to shift one's position without carrying anything else. One garment additional to flying gear was the pair of coarse woollen 'long John's' issued to us to keep our lower limbs warm. They seemed to achieve this in some degree by their severe chafing and irritation. However, I shoved the gun down my flying boot and contemplated how easy it would be to terminate my earthly existence by emerging from a crashed aircraft in enemy held territory brandishing a gun.

We did an 'Adder' patrol, carrying rocket projectiles, screening the starboard flank of the convoy. Two hours airborne and I felt frozen stiff from feet to fingertips. I had difficulty in moving with any degree of ease particularly because of extreme discomfort in my bladder. Our patrol completed, we flew back towards *Nairana*. Sighting her, I estimated that I'd be down in twenty minutes. The time scale gave me a sort of relief. Then, a morse signal was flashed from the carrier —"Continue patrol for a further hour". That hour was purgatory to me. I was hardly able to move

Facing page: The 'Bluenose' certificate awarded to the author, October 1944.

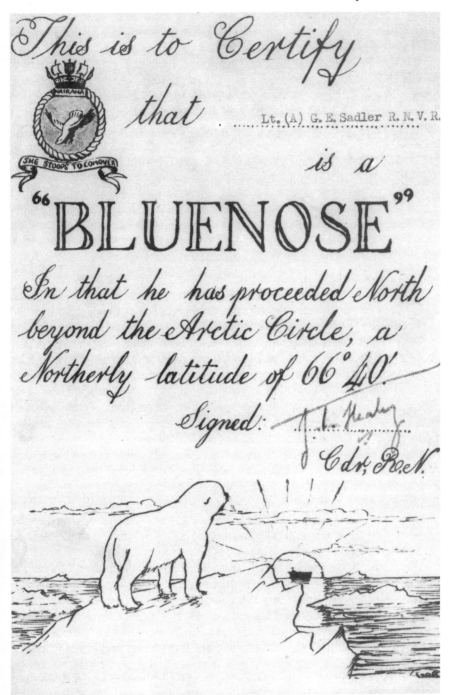

This is to Certify that ....Lt. (A) G. E. Sadler R. N. V. R.......... is a

"BLUENOSE"

In that he has proceeded North beyond the Arctic Circle, a Northerly latitude of 66° 40'.

Signed: ....

Cdr, R.e.N.

Three Swordfish aircraft, armed with practice bombs, awaiting take-off. Note the lower arrester wire in the foreground.

and felt extremely cold. After well over three hours, we returned to the carrier.

Never was I so relieved to complete a flight and land on safely. I had to be assisted out of the aircraft. The other two planes returned and both crashed on the deck. Fortunately the crews were uninjured. None of us detected any U-boats.

The CO and I were up again later the same day, or rather night, but our ASVX showed a fault which caused us to curtail our patrol to something over an hour which, fortunately did not reduce me to an icicle as before. I put down safely and go my head down as best I could in a ship that would not remain steady. I was never sick, though the constant unpredictable lurching movements certainly affected one's balance and induced headaches. There was no sanctuary from it excepting perhaps in the air but, as I have indicated, that was not unalloyed joy.

Tracker, an American built 'Banana Boat', was less stable in heavy seas than *Nairana* and *Vindex*, our British built escort carriers. Her wider deck availed her nothing. She managed at last to get her Grumman Avengers into the air. The weather had been so bad before, that the deck was too unsteady to range them and get them airborne, let alone for them to land back on the carrier. A sub' was spotted on the surface by the crew of one Avenger but it dived before an effective attack could be made with the depth charges carried.

Vindex took the last period of duty as we sailed through the channel between the minefields and into Kola Inlet close by Murmansk.

We were allowed ashore, but there was little to see. German bombing had destroyed most of the buildings. The residents dwelt in rudimentary accommodation and eked out an existence on meagre basic rations. Although they were not unfriendly, it was difficult to converse with the Russians because of our ignorance of their language and their ignorance of ours. We had some Russian officers on board to entertain them. They ate voraciously as though they had been deprived of anything approaching good food. The bread rolls on the table, of white flour, disappeared like magic once they were seated. Drinks of any wine or spirit went 'down the hatch' in one gulp. Before we sailed out escorting a convoy homeward bound, men of the Red Fleet gave us a concert of music and dance in the aircraft hangar. It was magnificent in every respect.

Our return on 2nd November started with a sad loss. Knowing that there were many U-boats lurking outside the mouth of the Kola Inlet awaiting the convoy, the escort vessels set sail to oppose them before the convoy assembled. We dispatched no U-boats, but they sank one of our frigates, HMS *Mountsey*. That most unhappy incident behind us, we got under way.

On our return trip, sea conditions deteriorated so that the heavy Avengers could not always be ranged. *Vindex* had an unfortunate time experiencing some losses of, and damage to, aircraft and a fault with the aircraft lift. Consequently, it's full rota of flying duties could not be properly fulfilled. Eventually, judging weather conditions to be unsuitable, the Vice Admiral called flying off altogether.

The signal to *Nairana* to cease flying was questioned by Captain Surtees. He advised the Vice Admiral that he could fly. That, you'll understand, was not a personal assertion. It meant that the CO, Val Jones and I flew off into the darkness to discover if flying was possible. We proved that it was by doing so. The combination of Val's navigation and my flying brought us safely back at a time when the sea swell was such that one massive roll took *Nairana* to a measured 54 degrees. The situation in the hangar was chaotic. It needed but one aircraft to break from the securing fitments on the deck for it to run amuck and damage all our complement of planes and seriously injure the maintenance crews. Many had sustained minor but painful injuries when manhandling the folded aircraft into position. Our patrol over, the other crews followed where we had led. Val and I continued with night flying patrols. There were some deck landing accidents with other pilots, one aircraft being a write off, but we lost no crews, though *Nairana* continued protective patrols until we were near enough to Shetland for cover to be provided by the RAF Coastal Command.

It was with some pride that we sailed through driving snow down the West coast of Scotland and into the Clyde, not having lost any merchant ships either outward or homebound — a rare achievement to Russia. We, *Nairana*, were complimented by the Vice Admiral. Presumably Captain Surtees had made his point. 835 Squadron certainly had. There was but moral support from our fighter pilots who, rather frustrated, never got into the air. On reflection, they were perhaps lucky. They of course stood ready. "They also serve..."

Chapter 14 — Fond Farewells

The squadron was granted nine days leave, well earned we thought. I was surprised to be given fifteen days leave and orders to report to 798 Squadron at HMS *Daedalus*, Lee on the Solent, for a monoplane conversion course.

It was an odd feeling to be leaving 835 Squadron. I had served in it for two years and seven months. During that time I had flown on and off seven aircraft carriers. I had done 207 deck landings, more than any other pilot, though Bob Selley reached that same number four months later. I also got in a hundred more flying hours than any other pilot achieved with the squadron.

I packed together my belongings, including the personal touches spread around the cabin — the cabin which I had shared with Stan Thomas and, after Stan's departure, with Al Burghham. It was a comfortable billet about a quarter ship's length starboard from the stern, appreciably above the water line and with a port. Al chose to move in with me, being enamoured with both the port and my company. We got on well.

Parting from friends was something of a wrench, particularly in Val Jones' case. Our understanding and confidence in each other had been superb. We calmly got on with the job and our results were rewarding. Having said my goodbyes to the squadron fellows, our maintenance crews and the ship's officers, I wanted to get off to catch the night train from Glasgow, but felt that I should first report my departure to Captain Surtees. He was late coming in for dinner, so I had the rashness to go to his cabin and knock on the door. An angry voice bid me enter. I did so. He wasn't expecting me. I saw him in quite a new light. Whilst I was smoothly turned out, he was not. He was perched on the side of his bunk attired in what had been his only clean white shirt, underpants and socks. Shaving with undue haste or with an imperfect blade, a not uncommon hazard in wartime, he had thrice cut his face and was unsuccessfully endeavouring to staunch the flow of blood, which had transformed his upper garment into something resembling an imperfect white ensign. He left swearing, thrust away the shirt and did his best to express his satisfaction with my service and wish me well. The interview was of short duration. He was not a socialiser at the best of times. This was not the best of times and my sartorial elegance put him rather at a disadvantage. Besides, he was mighty late for dinner.

I nevertheless left 835 Squadron and *Nairana* with a glowing report from Captain Surtees. He held my performance as a pilot and as a naval officer in the highest esteem. I was contented that I had survived some difficult situations and earned the respect of two captains.

My welcome leave over, I repaired to my conversion courses with 798 Squadron as ordered. The intention was to familiarise me with the characteristics of monoplanes, particularly the Barracuda, the British made reconnaissance torpedo bomber, successor to the Swordfish. I commenced the courses in a Miles master, a training plane I'd not flown before. It was a tricky aircraft to fly, its propensity to stall without warning, if critical airspeeds were not observed, was paramount. This marvellously concentrated one's mind on the job. It was a change from the Stringbag. One advanced the throttle, there was an immediate response from the engine and 'hey presto', you were off. From the Master I went onto Fairey Fulmars doing general flying and aerobatics, then onto the Barracuda.

I did some routine flying, then tried a slow roll which was easy to do with an unloaded plane, then advanced to doing some diving with and without flaps and carrying a dummy torpedo. How disappointing was the performance. I found that it was quite impossible to keep pace with a Dakota! The aircraft was so heavy that the engine had too much to do. The Barracuda was reputed to be a good dive bomber but I yearned for something better. The course took three weeks. Now what? More leave, but what then?

I travelled home to Manchester via London. There I had the temerity to visit Queen Anne's Mansions, where NA2SL, the Fleet Air Arm Drafting Unit, was housed. It was understood that one had to be a Lieutenant Commander to grace its portals, but I chanced my arm. Having enquired and found the proper office, I entered and introduced myself to a Lieutenant Commander, RN, who appeared to be in charge and asked if he might give me a hint of where I would be sent next. He turned up my records and enquired what courses I had done, though, as he'd got the records, I reckon that he should have known. I reeled them off — Torpedo Dropping, Deck Landing, Catapult, Instrument Flying, Western Approaches, Rocket Projectile, Safety Equipment, Rocket Assisted Take Off and Barracuda Conversion courses.

He conceded that I had done all the relevant courses for a TBR pilot, he could think of no more and said that I would probably be drafted to Ronaldsway in the Isle of Man, there to give operational instruction on Barracudas. It was the last thing I wanted to do. I had longed to get to fly on Fireflies, in a warmer theatre of war than the inhospitable Atlantic Ocean. I therefore made objection to the suggestion, saying that I did not consider it a good idea for me to undertake operational instruction on an aircraft of which I had no operational experience and, indeed, had flown for but fifteen hours. He, the Lieutenant Commander, put it to me that I was afraid of the aircraft. I seem to have a knack of disagreeing with my senior officers, but I was not prepared to take that, especially as I had formulated the opinion that my informant, from his uniform badges, was a chairborne character. We had words — strong words! The conversation was terminated. We did not part the best of friends. I came away irritated and ignorant of what might befall.

It got me Christmas and New Year leave and a bit more. Enquiring neighbours, round about my home, wondered aloud when I was returning to fight the war. It was the longest leave I had during my service — something like four weeks. Eventually, orders came that I was to report to the RAF No 3 Instructors School at Lulsgate Bottom, Bristol to undergo a full flying instructors course. Apparently I'd not had enough courses. Thoughts of a warmer theatre of war were pipe dreams. It seemed that "Chairborne" was determined to make me an instructor at all costs.

Lulsgate Bottom was a misnomer, because the airfield was situated on high ground. My course there was during a spell of severe wintry weather with much snow and freezing temperatures. Accommodation was in a wretched nissen hut large enough to house seventy, but occupied by less than a dozen. Its total heating consisted of a coke burning contraption situated in the middle of the hut. It contributed virtually nothing towards raising the interior temperature above the outdoor temperature. The ablutions were across a snow covered field where one had the luxury of washing and shaving in cold water — just above freezing. One attended what passed for breakfast with a rosy complexion! I was so affronted by the facilities afforded by the RAF, as was the other naval Lieutenant on the course, an RN officer from another squadron, that when the airfield became unsuitable for flying we fled. We were so miserably cold and uncomfortable, that we bussed our way to the Lamb Hotel at Axbridge and spent a couple of nights there. It was a fascinating ancient hostelry with cobbles up to the bar and an old skittle alley behind. But — to the course.

I found myself back on Harvards also on Masters. This time I was learning how to fly aircraft very correctly so as to be able to explain what I was intending to do and how I operated the controls to achieve it. The next step was to develop the skill and patience to impart that knowledge to others and to train them. Over the previous three years I had been flying, using my experience and initiative to meet the flying conditions. I had operated the aircraft controls automatically and instinctively without having to think about it. The business of talking through what one was doing was foreign to me. In early March, with perseverance, I completed the course and was awarded a category C certificate as a single engined aircraft flying instructor.

I learned to my sorrow, that Johnny Hunt, who left 835 Squadron before me and attended the Flying Instructor's School, had lost his life in a flying accident here. It appeared that I was the first ex 835 Squadron pilot to complete the course and qualify. Having done ten courses covering every one a TBR pilot could do — plus a flying instructor's certificate, I wondered where I would be sent to next. It took ten days for me to be ordered back to join 798 Squadron at HMS *Daedalus*, Lee on Solent, as a flying instructor.

Chapter 15 — The Certified Instructor

798 Squadron, under the command of Lt Cdr Wallace, was unique in that it was the only naval squadron with certified instructors. In all there were about a dozen of us, mostly ex operational, some fighter pilots, some TBR pilots. Amongst them I found my friend Frank Cowtan, whom I had last met in 833 Squadron. The others were new to me.

It was not quite clear which way the squadron was to develop. In all flying training, elementary, intermediate and advanced, the Navy was dependent upon RAF Training Schools. Operational training was undertaken by the Navy. We were given to understand that the intention was for the Navy to undertake its own training ab initio once a full working unit had been established. During my service, until I was demobilised in early '46, this did not happen. Instead, we were employed on giving refresher courses and conducting tests with pilots sent to us from operational squadrons by their commanding officers to assess their flying abilities and detect their faults. These activities, I gather, continued as the main function of 798 Squadron. It became known as 'The Trappers'.

Daedalus was the HQ, the Mecca of the Fleet Air Arm. My accommodation was in a well furnished roomy cabin which I shared with 'Guffy' Birch. Everything was kept immaculate by the Wren stewards. Messing was first class in the huge impressive dining room, meals on Sundays occasionally being served to the strains of the Royal Marine Band ensconced in the entrance like a palm court orchestra. Being a Lieutenant, I was entitled to use the wardroom, which gave me comfort and quiet away from the more junior officers noisy behaviour in the Gun Room.

Aircraft were dispersed round the airfield, not secured in hangars. We had a range of planes — Harvards, Masters, Fulmars, Barracudas, Fireflies, an Avenger and a Seafire. Being involved in testing, which necessitated flying dual with visiting pilots, most of our work was done in Harvards, there being more of them than there were Masters. They were also more reliable.

One mode of transport that was once more back into its own was my bicycle. It had started its service at Lee on Solent and now returned there in great shape some three years later. It saved me much legwork in getting from the officers quarters to and from the Squadron Office which was on the opposite side of the airfield. Quite properly, being a naval vehicle, it was a Raleigh. From late March on we enjoyed good weather throughout the Summer. There was plenty of work to do and I was often airborne three times in a day as well as being in charge of three or four pilots. We did no night flying, so our evenings were free, apart from our being required the usual station officer duties which were not onerous. To make life even more pleasant, there was no enemy bombing of the Portsmouth area as there had been in '41. We could sleep o'nights.

In the operational squadron I had been used to having another job outside my flying duties. In 798 Squadron there were none. Bertie Birse organised things, being the senior officer under Wallace. He allocated the incoming pilots to instructors. We arranged our programmes with him. This was satisfying, because we worked under our own initiative. I made my own reports.

I was keen on sport as was Guffy. Within the curtilage of *Daedalus* there were two little used tennis courts. We changed that. Many an evening, after flying, 'G' and I played singles until we raised a sweat, went for a shower, changed and had dinner. After dinner we strolled down to that fine pub, the *Victoria*, where our pewter tankards were kept behind the bar, had a drink and strolled back, calling by way of the kitchens where the wren stewards thoughtfully left any overage of savouries from dinner in the ovens for us to pillage. There was some scrunching as we unavoidably trod in the darkness on the crawling cockroaches on the tile floor but, being replete and contented, it did not worry us. Beside the pub was a splendid soccer pitch, surrounded, not by any spectators structure, but by imposing mature trees. Here we played some matches in which 'G' and I turned out.

My interest in leisure activities caused me to wonder about the other ranks. Enquiry revealed that no officer was responsible for or interested in what they did. I pursued the matter and got myself designated as Squadron Sports Officer. This proved rewarding. My persistence in researching into things resulted in my uncovering the existence of grants available to procure sports equipment. Unfortunately, like so many of these kind of things, the squadron lost out somewhat because some of the opportunities were time expired. However, I did what I could and the ratings were soon the proud possessors of a complete set of cricket gear amongst other things. Not that I, or any of the officers, played the game. Come to think of it, only Guffy and I participated in any sport. The others disdained any exertion.

It was possible to bathe in the sea close to the air station. There was a decent beach and clear water so, providing the water was warm enough, I sometimes took exercise that way at weekends. *Daedalus* being a large establishment, we had ENSA entertainments of good quality from time to time. All in all I applied myself to my job conscientiously, but also lived the life of an officer and a gentleman. After the privations of life in stormy seas it was luxury. The company was good and members of the squadron got on harmoniously.

On a personal note, I was able to get some attention that had escaped me during my operational service. One concern was trouble with my sinuses occasioned by my breaking my nose some four years earlier and not receiving proper attention at that time. I attended the naval hospital at Haslar, but the treatment did not prove efficacious. More satisfying was my finding the dental unit, where a skilled and most charming RN Commander took the time to examine and give the necessary

The author as a Sub Lieutenant, RNVR. Note the 'A' for 'Air' in the loop of the rank insignia with the pilots wings above it.

attention to my teeth. He took pains to check everything carefully and dismissed me with my mouth in perfect condition. His remedial work probably contributed to my having my own teeth today. Not a full set, but good enough!

Another problem, when one had become an itinerant as a naval officer, was one's washing. We wore white shirts and stiff collars, though we sometimes got away with *Van Heusen* collars if we could acquire them. This set a problem and, although we did some of our own dhobiing, we were to a large degree dependent upon laundry services. At Lulsgate Bottom such services were essential, hot water at that wretched station being unavailable. In the time honoured habit of laundries, the clothes were never laundered and ready for collection at the promised time so, not surprisingly, I found myself at Lee on Solent whereas my last batch of laundry was at Lulsgate Bottom. Repeated requests that it be forwarded to me were not heeded and eventually I fell back on the old maxim that if you wanted something doing, do it yourself.

Disregarding what I assumed to be the rule by not making enquiry about it, I got a Firefly fuelled and obtained clearance to fly to Lulsgate on laundry patrol. After all I arranged my own flying programme. My intended trip must have been advertised, because Third Officer Hall, one of the Wren officers on the station, heard of it and beseeched me to divert and take her as a passenger to Charmy Down, near Bath. She'd got some leave and the lift would assist her considerably. Although reluctant to compound the irregularity of my trip, under pressure I agreed to oblige her. I got her into the rear cockpit in the appropriate flying safety gear and set course for Charmy Down, a small airfield. The flight was straightforward. I landed, taxied to the Air Watch Office, switched off, gave the lady a hand out, returned to my cockpit and waved goodbye.

I did not go anywhere. The aircraft engine refused to fire. Pressing the starter button achieved nothing.

It is at times like these that the enormity of one's misdeeds parade themselves before you. I should not have been near to Bath, nor at Lulsgate for that matter. My mind turned over the consequences of an enquiry into my self authorised activities. Not being an aircraft mechanic, I was not au fait with Firefly maintenance, but I had formulated the opinion that the fault lay with the cartridge holder's not rotating properly so that there was no cartridge into line when I pressed the button for it to turn over the engine. I got out of the aircraft, stood on a wheel and clambered on to the wing to reach the panel under which the equipment was housed. I could not remove it. I walked to the Air Watch Office went in and requested the loan of a screwdriver. Miraculously they'd got one. I returned to the plane and dislodged the panel. As I suspected, the magazine had not fully rotated after the last cartridge was fired. I gave it a thump. It turned into line. I replaced the panel, returned the screwdriver, boarded the aircraft, pressed the tit and she fired.

I breathed a great sigh of relief, but carried things off quite well. My activities had excited some interest and the ground staff at Charmy Down had not seen a naval pilot repair a Firefly with a screwdriver before. They were suitably impressed and I did nothing to indicate that my desperate fault finding exercise was inspired guess work and not normal run of the mill stuff.

My flight to Lulsgate was short. I landed, taxied to the Control Tower parked the plane and found my laundry which was held there awaiting my arrival. Returning to the Firefly I found that I had company. Several of the flying school instructors were examining the aircraft and all of them clamoured to have a trial flight. I'd had enough for one day and managed to damp their enthusiasm. Apart from exchanging pleasantries, I eschewed conversation, got myself airborne again without any trouble and returned to *Daedalus* PDQ. I don't recall having the need to demonstrate my engineering prowess again.

One day I quite inadvertently came close to deep trouble. *Nairana* finished her tour of duty. 835 Squadron was wound up and the crews dispersed. A number of the other ranks came ashore to *Daedalus*. I met some of them and was invited to join them for pre prandial drinks in the Petty Officers Mess at lunchtime. It was not a party but simply a personal invitation. It was kind of them so I agreed to look in at the PO's Mess after my morning flying. I peddled over from the Squadron Office to the PO's place on my cycle where I was well received. In no time we were reminiscing about *Nairana* days. Somebody provided me with a half pint tumbler into which he had poured some rum — Navy rum. Petty Officers drew their daily rum ration neat. It was a marvellous pure — something over proof sprit, but easy and smooth on the palate. As other ex *Nairana* POs came in they topped up my glass so that I, being deeply occupied in swapping yarns, quite unwittingly consumed about half a pint of the powerful potion. Reckoning that it was time that I left for lunch, I made my farewells and was asked a question. "Are you flying this afternoon, Sir?" I replied in the affirmative, indicating that I must be off so as to lunch and return to the Squadron Office in time for my afternoon programme. There appeared to be some veiled humour in the company which I could not comprehend. My final goodbyes said, I opened the door. The fresh air assailed me. At once my faculties cleared and I realised that I had overdone the drinking. Unfortunately the condition of the members of my body did not follow suit. I managed to mount my fixed wheel steed at the third attempt and started for the Officers Mess being cheered on by a group of ex *Nairana* POs in the doorway of their mess who were convulsed with laughter.

About thirty yards on my way and I was saluted by a rating. I endeavoured to return the salute and, losing control of my vehicle ploughed into a flower bed and dismounted in an untidy heap amongst the plants. The Commander's block lay ahead to my left. Mercifully, it being lunchtime it was deserted. I rammed my cap on my head, seized the bike and rode hell for leather along the road round the back of the Officer's block and straight into the cycle rack. Strangely, being anaesthetised, I did myself no injury performing that risky manoeuvre.

Sometime around six o'clock, I stirred and came to. I was lying on my bunk in my cabin. There was an overpowering stench of rum and I could hear voices. One said "George is coming round now". I rose unsteadily to find that I'd got company, there being three or four officers in the room. "Come on," said Guffy, "get organised, were going out". A jolly good swill and brush up, a gathering of my garments, which were strewn about the room in disarray and I got dressed. A mirror examination reflected that I didn't look too bad. The odd thing was that I didn't feel bad or sickly. There was no sign whatever of a hangover. I joined the crew and went out with them having no ill effects from my overindulgence.

The situation that befell me was one with which we had trouble at times. Its description on the lower deck was 'Birthday Tots', which meant that, on a fellow's birthday, his pals all surrendered their daily ration to him usually rendering him paralytic. Years ago Admiral Vernon, whose regular turnout was a suit of Grogam Tweeds, decreed that ranks below Petty Officer should have their daily rum ration watered down to discourage drunkenness. The diluted spirit was referred to as "grogged". Being in the Petty Officers Mess my rum wasn't.

I didn't make the same mistake again. Mind you, I didn't get the opportunity. Nobody can do so now. Today's Royal Navy is dry!

Still on a personal note, a very personal note, the question arose as to whether I was to marry my fiancee during hostilities or wait until the war was over. We had been courting for long enough. My parents, being very possessive over their only child, did not favour my marrying at all, regardless of who the young lady be. When I went home on leave they did their utmost to monopolise my time so that even courting gave rise to difficulties and privacy was at a premium. Dorothy and I had a serious discussion. It got to the point that either we got wed or called the whole thing off. We reached the decision to marry towards the end of 1945 whether the war be over or not. We did not think that it would be over by then. That resolved, we communicated our decision to our parents.

On the war front things moved quickly after that. We felt that we'd hurried things up! May brought VE Day and much rejoicing at *Daedalus*.

I recall the unanimous unannounced decision that work ceased, though as we were fed in the mess, presumably that sentiment did not extend to everybody. At any rate there was no flying. After a leisurely breakfast, Guffy and I walked down to the Victoria which seemed to have disregarded licensing laws and had opened betimes. We had a jar, then returned to *Daedalus* armed with our personal tankards. The Mess, a commodious room, was full of people. I soon found myself embraced by a senior officer Paymaster who poured spirit into my flagon and behaved like a father welcoming his prodigal son. Fortunately he did not hold me in his fond embrace over long, finding another to love. Sundry officers I knew not seemed fascinated with my tankard, not desiring it, but to ensure that it was kept filled. As the announcement had been made to 'Splice the Mainbrace', spirits flowed freely and indiscriminately. I can assert that the only liquor not contained in my tankard was beer, the brew for which surely it was intended. Some idiot brought our noisy good natured rejoicings to an abrupt conclusion by setting off a smoke float containing titanium tetrachloride in the mess. Its nauseous fumes drove everybody out of the room and the perpetrator was roundly condemned.

My memory of the later events of that day are hazy. I do recall entering a cinema either in Portsmouth or Fareham and seeing the film *Henry V*. My attention wandered. I was grateful to be seated and felt exhausted. It was a mite difficult to come to terms with the situation. The war in Europe was over. I had survived. I must confess, like others, of being rather selfish in not extending my thoughts to consider the situation of our comrades in the Far East. May we be excused. Our festivities were spontaneous and I think understandable.

The historic day was over, next morning we repaired to our flying fatigues.

On our duties in 798 Squadron we met a fair cross section of naval pilots. Some were on the conversion course from Swordfish to Barracudas, some sent to us by their commanding officers for our assessment of their abilities. The second group were unknown quantities and could give rise to alarming experiences.

One young man of the assessment group, he was a Sub Lieutenant flying TBR aircraft in an operational squadron, did not endear himself to me. He was conceited and overconfident, advised me that he'd got a job lined up with a commercial airline for his post war profession and seemingly had the conviction that he'd come to give me some instruction on flying. I wondered if his commanding officer had told him of the purpose of his being sent to us. I put my prejudice aside and said that we'd do some dual flying in a Harvard. He had flown Harvards and pronounced himself conversant with them. I gave him the handbook on the plane to refresh his memory. He soon declared himself familiar with all he required to know, so we got airborne.

Under my instruction he did some general flying, simple aerobatics and forced landing procedures reasonably but in a careless manner. When we came to land he did not observe the proper approach speed and, in spite of my prompting, neglected to correct it so that we were appreciably below the speed that should have been maintained. I told him to go round again and perform a text book landing — one according to the handbook. He did the same thing again, then again. I reminded him that the tolerance of the Harvard was peculiar to that aircraft. It did not extend to others. If he disregarded the instructions on the handling notes of other aircraft he would court disaster. My comments were treated with disdain. I tried another tack. I said that we'd fly in a Miles Master. Had he knowledge of that aircraft? Yes, he knew all about it. I left him to study the handbook and made sure that he'd done so before we took to the air again.

The Master demanded more precise flying than the Harvard. It needed little below the designated airspeed for it to stall. When it did so, it gave no forewarning. A wing dropped in an instant and the plane would go out of control. From the instructor's point of view I did not care for them. In the rear cockpit one could see little and to get a view of the runway on landing one had to raise the perspex canopy and stretch one's head above the fuselage. Our Masters were rather clapped out and they leaked oil from the radial engine. This to some degree spattered over the windscreen. That did not help. All prepared, we had another flight after I had warned the pilot that flying with a cavalier disregard of airspeeds in a Master were not to be recommended.

We taxied out, did the drill for take off and took to the air. After a short period of local flying, I asked my assessee if he could do a loop — the most straightforward of aerobatics. He said he could, so I asked that he should go ahead and do one, first climbing to eight thousand feet. That caused him to make objection. Why should he climb to that height? It wasn't necessary and so on. I was obdurate, also I was in charge. I told him to do as I said. Having attained the altitude I wanted, I invited him to go ahead.

The Sub Lieutenant performed as I had anticipated. So did the Master. We got to the top of the loop, the airspeed dropped too low and we did a high speed stall. In next to no time we were down to four thousand feet. As my driver didn't seem to be doing anything to remedy the situation, I decided to take things in hand and follow the standard recovery procedure.

Having I thought, learned his lesson I got him on a little more general flying, then asked him to land. I emphasised the importance of maintaining the correct airspeed on the approach and landing, reminding him what it was. We approached, I with the canopy raised and my shoulders level with the upper body of the plane. The flaps were lowered, the undercarriage went down and so did the airspeed! My exhortations over the RT to maintain speed evoked no response. I shouted instructions to no avail.

A difficult decision for an instructor is to determine when, in a dual controlled aircraft, to take over control. The pupil is often waiting for you to do so and can feel the movement of the aircraft's controls in his cockpit if you do take over. The instructor is trying to get his pupil to do the correct thing. If as, in this case, the pilot is trained sufficiently to be appointed to a first line squadron he should be capable of doing so.

My decision came at the very last moment. Even as I thrust the throttle forward through to the override position and eased back on the stick the starboard wing dropped like a stone. The Master executed a vertical turn, wheels and flaps down only twenty feet above the chequered van at the end of the runway. I recovered sufficient speed to remain airborne, just, and steered an unorthodox course across the airfield until I could climb to a proper height. I then did a regular circuit and landed the aircraft myself, being thankful to be alive. I had experienced dangerous situations in foul weather and on stormy seas but not on a fine sunny day on a good airfield.

I will not reveal a word of my report. Suffice it to recall that I had piloted TBR aircraft for two and a half years in an operational squadron. The lives of my observer and air gunner had been dependent upon my flying knowledge and ability and on my applying myself assiduously to the job in hand, bearing in mind my responsibilities to them.

The example I give is but one of many potentially dangerous situations with which an instructor may at times be confronted. A pupil freezing on the controls is a harassing experience. Fortunately in 798 Squadron I was not beset with too many of these untowards happenings.

It was with considerable distaste that I found one trainee allocated to me. He had completed his elementary flying course and was to go to Canada for his intermediate and advanced flying on Harvard aircraft. The intention of his being placed with 798 Squadron was that he be introduced to Harvards and do some flying in them, thus gaining an advantage over the other members of his course. I considered it to be quite improper and unfair. The trainee was the son of a Vice Admiral. My memory still serves me, but I decline to recall the name though the subterfuge sickened me.

With a marriage to discuss and little opportunity to discuss it, I arranged a clandestine way of doing so. Having been given permission to take some leave, I decided to find a suitable place for a holiday, neglect to tell my parents that I had been granted leave and arrange that Dorothy and I have a clear week to ourselves. I thought of Devon.

Scanning my local airfield map, I found that a landing field was shown on the coast close to Teignmouth. Around there would do. I arranged my programme so that a pupil should do a cross country flight to Devon for exercise, with me as a passenger. I reckoned there was little danger of his getting lost returning solo to Lee on Solent, which was on the coastline.

We boarded a Harvard and set of. There was no problem until we reached our destination, which proved to be a small rough field near the cliff edge. The only hint that an aircraft might land on it was that there was a windsock — not that there was any wind. The noise of our aircraft brought the sole occupant of the landing field to life. Out of what resembled a garden shed tumbled a bell bottomed rating. Because of the nature of the terrain I resolved to land the plane myself and by doing a couple of low circuits I managed to convey to the fellow of my intention. He returned to his bothy and emerged with an Aldis lamp with which he flashed a green light. I used the longest approach the field afforded and landed. I got out of the plane, selected the best possible run for a take off for my pupil and bid him return to Lee, taking the utmost care in getting airborne. It was a longish run before he achieved lift off and I was much concerned until he managed to get unstuck. The field was far from a bowling green consistency and the aircraft trundled and bounced over the hummocks for what seemed an eternity before it was up and away. That achieved, my prayers answered, I searched for and found an hotel at Shaldon where I booked a holiday.

There was a disconcerting incident to get over the following day. I had to be back at *Daedalus*, giving no indication that I had ever been away. To this end, I had arranged that an instructor friend flew over and picked me up. At the agreed time I stood on the 'airfield', for want of a more appropriate name, and waited. An Anson aircraft arrived, flew overhead a couple of times, and, by its manoeuvres, gave me the conviction that it was not going to land. I made frantic signals to the pilot. My antics induced him to approach and, very gingerly to put down. He was not happy and was only induced to land because of my predicament if he didn't and because I had demonstrated that it could be done by my landing the Harvard. I scrambled aboard, wondering where the Anson had been discovered. I didn't know that we'd got one. A maximum possible run, more prayers to the Almighty, dual on this occasion, an uneven progression over the rutted greensward and we managed to get on our way. I thanked my friend, who must have weighed the odds carefully, because he was a trainee barrister. He cursed me. I reminded him that we could do the impossible to order if required.

Encouraged by my organisational success, I tried one thing more. It was time consuming travelling from Lee on Solent to my home near Manchester. 'Wings' at *Daedalus*, Lt Cmdr Robertson, was on leave at his home at Wilmslow, close by Ringway Airport and due to return about the same time as my leave commenced. He readily approved of my proposal that I fly a Firefly to Ringway and that he fly it back. The plan worked out nicely. It took me but forty minutes from take off to landing at economical weak mixture cruising as opposed to the public service travel

— bus to Gosport, ferry to Portsmouth, Portsmouth to London, cross London, London to Manchester with the difficulty of making connections it took the best part of a day. Surprising how one may be granted a concession if it is to the benefit of the senior officer who conceded it.

Our holiday went quite well. We enjoyed good weather. The hotel was populated largely by bejewelled elderly ladies who cherished the establishment as a refuge from wartime discomforts. The head waiter was arrogant and rude. He rated us as something akin to the 'Bisto Kids' because, during the day, I was attired in shorts and very casual wear and robed myself in tidy but much worn civilian clothing for evening meals. The food was poor. What one did not rise to consuming one day, became next day's 'Cabinet Pudding'. The only other serviceman was a ground crew RAF Sergeant who seemed to rate as an important person akin to royalty. What I was and how I came to be there was obviously the subject of much speculation. It suited us well. We wanted peace and quiet. On our final night at the hotel I entered the dining room in my naval lieutenant's uniform. The impact it had on the other diners was most amusing. The waiter became most obsequious, behaved in a manner a head waiter should and almost grovelled for a reward in respect of his services — too late I fear!

For our part we sorted out our marriage arrangements to our satisfaction and enjoyed the holiday on the basis of 'two's company...'.

One group of naval officers who came to 798 I greatly admired. They were the ex prisoners of war, those RN pilots who had been taken prisoner rather than losing their lives at the outset of the war. The planes they flew were Fairey Battles — vulnerable, lumbering aircraft. Opposed to them were Messerschmitt 109s. It was a non contest between the two aircraft. Unable to outmanoeuvre the 109s and too slow to make their escape, the naval pilot's only hope was to fly very low over the water. A fighter attacking from above ran the risk of following through into the sea. It was a forlorn hope for many. The officers who came to us had survived but were taken prisoner.

They were intelligent, handsome, surprisingly buoyant and eager to busy themselves with a refresher course so as to take to the air again in modern planes and continue with their duties. Their main regret was the time that had been wasted during their sojourn in POW camps. It had interfered with their promotion.

They made me feel ashamed in one respect. During their spell in captivity they had seen to it that they exercised and kept fit. For my part, as I have related, I kept reasonably active, played soccer, tennis and swam. One game the ex POWs had played in their camps was basketball, which I had never tried. As the Sports Officer they considered that I should be into everything. I alone out of 798 Squadron attended the gym to be introduced to the game. In no time at all I was breathless and found myself running around aimlessly without being able to handle the ball. I was taken in hand, taught how to read the game, how to position myself and how to pass an opponent. Some moves I was made to do time and time again, half an hour at a time, repeatedly receiving the ball, turning, passing a defensive player and putting the ball in the net. It taught me a lot. With constant practice I was able to perform moves which I had thought impossible and I became quite proficient at the game. To improve, one had to work hard at it. Some players had a natural athletic ability much above the average. I hadn't. Nevertheless, with regular and constant application I became quite a decent player.

The group were very keen on their refresher flying course. They were a rewarding crew to instruct. They kept us on our mettle — no bad thing.

Another ex 835 Squadron member, John Defrates, joined 798 and we renewed our acquaintance. He like the rest of our squadron, excluding Guffy Birch, was not a sporting type but more an intellectual.

One thing we had in common was our political outlook. This was diametrically opposed to the general view of the wardroom at *Daedalus* which was staunchly true blue Conservative. We took care not to ventilate our opinions, especially if senior officers were within earshot, but there came a time when we surfaced. We sat in the wardroom, ears glued to the radio, rejoicing as we listened avidly to the Labour landslide election results coming through in July. Our expressed enthusiasm over the results as we congratulated each other was observed with obvious displeasure by the large majority of officers. They were too shaken to pause and hear the outcome of the voting. We, John and I, did not make ourselves conspicuous in the same way again. As it happened, a Sub Lieutenant at *Daedalus* stood for election and was elected as the Labour Party MP for my home constituency — mind you, he was RNVR.

The following month, August, the war was properly over. VJ Day was duly celebrated, not with the same sense of uninhibited relief as on VE Day, but with gratitude that we could turn our minds away from conflict and to the great task of repair and reconstruction. Our young lives had been disrupted by the hostilities. I had lost several of my close friends who had been in the forces. Our aspirations to achieve advancement in our civilian occupations had been stayed and there was much to do to reconcile ourselves to post war conditions and opportunities.

The war over, there was some serious thinking to be done about the future — my future. I stood in quite a favourable position in the navy. I was well qualified and experienced as a pilot and my 'flimsies', (so called because the copies that officers received were on very thin paper akin to greaseproof) the reports from my commanding officers, both on operations and in 798 Squadron, were very favourable. An odd, very irresponsible Sub Lieutenant who was at *Daedalus*, unconnected with us, took delight in displaying one of his reports to other officers for some unknown reason. The standard wording by the Captain, if he approved of his officer, read "During his Service under my command this officer has conducted himself to my entire satisfaction". There then followed any other remarks the Captain thought fit. The Sub Lieutenant, whose flimsy was produced for all to see, had stirred other sentiments in his commanding officer. It read "During his Service under my command this officer has conducted himself to his entire satisfaction". It was, you'll agree, deliciously worded, but it hardly resulted in a document in which to take pride.

I was offered a short service commission which gave reasonable prospects of promotion and a good chance of the command of a squadron in due course. The trouble was that I could not envisage service life as being acceptable to Dorothy after we were married. She had no experience of the forces. Also, my parents were not in the best of health and my father had become neurotic about my continued flying. My decision therefore was to return to civilian life.

That resolved, I considered what I might do. My friendship with Robin Shirley Smith and my observation of some of the work he did to keep his hand in during off duty hours had stimulated my interest in architecture. I had the conviction that I too could become an architect and enjoy the job. I made enquiry as to how one managed to enrol for a course of training. Being low on funds, I had made an allowance to my parents, I would have to be awarded a grant to maintain myself and my wife, though she had a job. Grants were being sought and approved, seemingly quite freely, and naval pilots were treated with favour. To my chagrin I was refused a grant. I was refused a grant, not just for an architectural course but for anything and everything. It seemed that, unlike other squadron officers, I'd had a job before I enlisted. I had not resigned from it when I joined the navy. The fact that the job was that of a sorting clerk and telegraphist in the General Post Office which paid me nothing, because the payment I received as a naval lieutenant with flying pay clearly exceeded the SC&T's pay, was regarded as no matter. Shirley, on his architectural course, could return to it, grant provided because he had not got a job. If I returned to civilian life, which I had resolved to do, I fell foul of a Ministry of Labour order which directed me back to my pre war job from which, on the plea of my father I had not resigned. "Don't give up your job lad, you'll regret it". Of course, when demobilised, I could resign from my Post Office employment, but I had no other job to go to, and no grant for a course of training would be made available. The ruling was outrageously unfair. I witnessed other officers getting assistance to study for the qualifications they sought. I felt hard done by. It crossed my mind later that I should have sought the help of my new constituency MP, but I was not brought up "to seek favours or to gain preferment over others by unfair influence". More fool me!

I put my bitter disappointment behind me with difficulty and got on with the job in hand. They were senior engineer officers who wished to learn how to fly. We'd got a good cross section now, because we also had some young pilots who for some reason had returned from overseas courses on Harvards and were in an 'in between' situation before being allocated to operational training establishments. 798 Squadron had become like the naval destroyer 'the maid of all work'.

We were comfortable at *Daedalus* but inevitably there was a change. Early in September with all manners of rumours afoot about the future of the squadron and its development, we were moved to Halesworth in Suffolk. I was not much impressed with the place, not Halesworth, but the airfield and its appointments. Originally the airfield was used by the US Air Force. Once they had run it down, their commander, who was of Irish extraction, and who hated the English, used a bulldozer to bury any useful piece of equipment they were discarding to deny the RAF the use of it. The RAF spent some short time in the place and departed leaving 'tail end Charlie', the Fleet Air Arm, to accept what was left. Compared to *Daedalus* it was poor and lacked creature comforts to which we had become accustomed.

Halesworth was an interesting market town with an imposing perpendicular church sited on a mound where the original Anglo Saxon church once stood. With a population of two thousand, other than the itinerant service procession, it boasted nineteen pubs! The railway, arriving mid nineteenth century, crossed the main road at right angles. An odd feature was that the road bisected the railway station platform. When a train stopped at or passed through Halesworth, a section of platform, standing about eight feet high, was shoved on its metal wheels into line so that it completely closed the road. Why the platform was not set to one side of the road and a level crossing established is beyond my understanding. Perhaps Halesworth sought to be unique in railway design.

On several occasions I attended morning service on the Sunday along with Willy Aston, one of our ex fighter pilot instructors. He joined the bell ringers and I sang in the choir. The rector's sermons were uninspiring. He was high church, dry and intellectual. His deliveries passed over the heads of the congregation who were mainly country folk. An intriguing regular member of the weekly assembly was the unkempt rustic who dozed throughout the services, his sole purpose in attending being to collect his loaf, part of a perpetual bequest made many years before by a local benefactor.

I did some persuading and cajoling with Willy's assistance. We arranged a turn out by a group of officers for Sunday matins. About twenty, half Wren officers and half naval pilots, cycled from the mess to the church one crisp autumn morning. The local populace witnessing this uncommon cavalcade showed surprised approval. After the service expressions changed as we mounted our cycles and rode the short distance to the nearest local pub. We all needed a drink after the sermon!

The local womens' institute members did their best to provide entertainment and hospitality to we naval types, particularly lower deck members. They sometimes got things slightly wrong. In my mind's eye I can still see the notice outside the village hall. 'TOM BOWLER' it announced in large letters. The description of what civilians call 'Bingo' seemed to have become confused with an old Sea Shanty!

On the flying front I received a shock. I was allocated four pupils and could not simultaneously give them personal attention. Whilst they were awaiting my flying with them, I sought to find them something to do. One of the 'in between' pilots, his Harvard course completed, I sent off to do some solo flying for a couple of hours. General flying, which I recommended, was to allow him to get the feel of things after his short lay off. It would include some map reading, simple aerobatics, forced landing practice and some circuits and landings. I got on with my other pupils.

Over two hours later alarm bells were sounding! The young man had not returned and the CO wanted to know why. As we helplessly wondered about his failure to return on time, I was questioned. "What was he sent up to do?" I had done nothing amiss, but I felt distinctly uncomfortable. Then some news filtered through. The aircraft had crashed.

We were apprised of the approximate position of the aircraft. In no time I had mounted the James motorcycle I used around the station and headed off cross country to find it, unmindful of the fact that I had neither licence nor insurance. Eventually, after some rough riding over farmland, I found the plane. One wing was in a field. The rest of the aircraft, inverted, was in the next field. The screen was smashed and there was blood upon it. The place was deserted. There was no sign of life.

I returned disconsolately to the Squadron Office feeling very upset. Further news was received. The pilot had been removed to hospital, apparently suffering from shock. His only injury was a cut forehead. That was all. I was greatly relieved.

Visiting my pupil later in hospital to enquire into his well being and being assured that he had but the one minor injury, I asked him what had happened. Advised by me that before performing aerobatics he should get plenty of altitude for safety, he had observed my instruction. I had also told him to try out some forced landings. The procedure for this was, on the presumption that one's engine had failed, to select a suitable place to make a forced landing, be it a field or a beach and glide to a position downwind of it. By gliding back and forth, remaining in a downwind position, one then reduced height until the altitude was such that one could turn into wind, make a glide approach and forced landing, undercarriage retracted, as gently as possible.

My pupil had combined the two exercises. He had climbed to ten thousand feet, to do aerobatics, higher than was strictly necessary. From that height he had decided, his aerobatics completed, to try a forced landing. A glide from ten thousand feet to something less than one thousand feet at the back end of the year with the throttle closed cooled the engine considerably. His selection of a suitable place for a forced landing was faulty as was his forced landing expertise. Having reduced height sufficiently to make his landing approach, he then advanced the throttle intending to fly off again. The Harvard, with its engine cold, demurred. It was then that my trainee realised that his selection of a suitable spot on which to put down was questionable, so was his forced landing technique. He was fortunate to be alive. I was most grateful that he was.

We had a bit of light hearted relief when we were requested to give a flying display at a civic ceremony at Southwold. It was according to the CO's, Bertie Birse's directions, Bertie had succeeded to commanding officer following Wallace's promotion to Commander and drafting elsewhere, to be a formation approach in Harvards. Some pretty formation stuff then break off into echelon at some height, dive till low over the civic dignitaries then alternate climbing rolls to left and right. "Not below two hundred feet" counselled 'B'. Fancy telling naval pilots that on a simulated beat up! We settled for twenty! Roy Gibb was to do some special manoeuvres in our Seafire because he was an outstanding aerobatic pilot. To my surprise I found, just before take off, that I'd got company. I was joined by an engineer commander who wished to come for the ride. We enjoyed ourselves, the populace of Southwold did, I think, once they had readjusted their headgear, and my commander passenger and I had uninhibited relief from the humdrum by hedge hopping our way back over the beautiful undulating country to tea in the mess.

There were no more personal alarms with my flying pupils. I interested myself in the squadron soccer team in which there were several good and keen players. I found that the station boasted a squash court, but we could not get the best use out of it. The walls had been painted with impermanent colour wash, consequently the balls became coloured as they struck it and were difficult to see. Also squash balls were very difficult to obtain as were rackets. The ex POWs were interested and we tried the court out but lack of resources and the courts needing repainting, defeated us. Basketball continued to be their game.

Chapter 16 — A Changed Status

The big event for October was my marriage to Dorothy. It took place in Urmston, our home town, on 30th October. Stan Thomas, my one time observer in 835 Squadron, with whom I had kept in touch, was the only Air Arm officer to attend. The 798 chaps had a whip round and gave us a gift of money. I carefully kept the money away from our urgent domestic demands and, in due course, used it to buy a beautiful cut glass and silver decanter, an antique, which graces our display cabinet and is used for special occasions. It has enhanced in value over the years. We newly weds spent one weeks honeymoon in Rhos on Sea, North Wales, the place in which we now live. Then we descended on Halesworth.

After some searching, we were able to arrange accommodation 'ashore' with the local vet and his wife, who had a large old property not far from the air station. My having the use of the James 125 motor cycle, made travelling for me simple. There were some difficulties over housekeeping arrangements with our being in 'digs', but they were not insurmountable and we began to settle down. Our main criticism was that the house, standing on an exposed cross road and having ill-fitting sash windows was cold regardless of from where the wind blew. Our life in our first 'home' did not last long. More precisely, it endured for about ten days!

I had arranged a coach for the 19th November to transport our football team to Great Yarmouth to play a match against another naval station. I was the only officer in the team. Having spare room on our coach, my new wife, who had discovered that one of her school friends was a Wren, stationed at Great Yarmouth, decided to travel, as did some supporters. On the journey I felt a bit off colour. When we got to our destination Dorothy followed up the arrangement to meet her friend and I prepared for the soccer match. I'm not the best traveller in coaches. God knows how I would have managed had I been an observer rather than a pilot, because sideways movement seems to affect my balance. Once out of the coach and into the fresh air, perishingly fresh cold air, I expected that all would be well. It wasn't! On the pitch I found that I was unable to run. There was a constricting feeling across my chest and I was unable to play a decent game. My inability to perform as anticipated gave rise to derisory comments from some team members. They questioned why I should have been considered for a place in the team. It was unkind, because I was a decent player, but I felt quite ill. I saw the game through even contributing to a cross from the right wing, to which position I had moved myself from centre half, onto the head of our bustling centre forward which gave us a draw. I managed to observe the courtesies, making the appropriate expressions of thanks to our hosts and crawled back aboard our transport in a collapsed condition. A good night's rest I hoped would see me well again. It was a pious hope, but to no avail. My night was disturbed with sickness and diarrhoea alternately and regularly. For newly weds it was hardly the way to get to know each other!

The morn, and I reported to the MO. He looked me closely in the eyes and diagnosed infective hepatitis — jaundice. He ordered that I be taken post haste to the isolation hospital some fifteen miles distant. An ambulance was my transport. There was no time afforded for man and wife to conclude any arrangements. I had to request the ambulance driver to stop thrice on our journey so that I might disgorge, the ambulance journey causing me to feel worse. Installed in the hospital, I was put on a fat free diet and caused to drink gallons of water and soft drinks. The treatment, seeming to consist of hydropathy, almost produced in me a state of hydrophobia as the over diligent nurse almost connected me to the ward tap! So persistent was she that we never made friends. I had other things on my mind. My wife of three weeks had been brought away from her home, housed with strangers in fairly spartan conditions, then deserted. I felt rotten. Anybody experiencing jaundice does.

Confined in an isolation hospital remote from everybody I knew, I felt desperately frustrated. There was so much to be done and I could contribute nothing. Nobody from the squadron visited me, but of course they were not meant to do so. Dorothy came twice, experiencing great difficulty with the rural transport, so we decided that it would be for the best if she returned to Manchester against my recovery. She had obtained three months leave of absence from her drawing office job in the aircraft factory so there was an element of flexibility over her movements beyond the year end.

Once she had left, I felt isolated in more than the medical sense. There was no news from the squadron, naught from Manchester and I was not blessed with good company in the other hospital patients. I was shrouded in a great wave of depression.

To my pleasure I received a letter from my mother. I recognised her writing upon the envelope. This was unusual, because she was not a scholar and did little writing. My father took pride in keeping up a regular and frequent correspondence. Sadly, his writings contained precious little news and the contents of his letters were predictable, though I was careful not to tell him so. Mother, on the other hand, packed quite a lot into a few lines so that one had to read carefully so as not to miss anything. I opened her letter with pleasure and interest. Both sentiments were short lived as I addressed myself to her message. It recommended that, as I lay on my sickbed, I reflect on what had brought me to this dreadful state. She was aware of the cause of jaundice — that it was ascribed to gross overindulgence of alcohol. I was given to understand that my self induced downfall was due to behaviour on the lines of *The Rakes Progress*. My mother having determined that a gross intake of alcohol was the sole reason for the onset of every form of jaundice, assumed that I had fallen from grace in every other depravity that she or I might bring to mind. I can assure all who have not experienced the effect of jaundice, that it is singularly flattening to mind and body. My dear caring mother, in one brief communication, improved on that situation so that I felt as if flattened by a road roller. I didn't bother to reply.

I had agonised over turning down a short service naval commission with good prospects, been refused a place on a training course for a subject I wished to study, was separated from my wife in but three weeks, was condemned by my mother for my loose living and felt absolutely drained and ill. I wondered where I had gone wrong.

Willy Aston had decided on demob' to study and take holy orders. He appeared to have set his star to rise. Mine had become unhooked from its heavenly support and lay low in the mire.

It was well into December before I was released from captivity. To simplify matters for me, during my incarceration, 798 Squadron had removed lock, stock and barrel across the country. I had the single handed task of gathering my things together from different places, no doubt losing some in the process and travelling from Halesworth via London to Manchester in frigid railway stock and freezing conditions. When one moved by public transport, one had to obtain travel vouchers so there was need to call at the naval air station as well as at my lodgings. My arrival in Manchester, my advent one might say bearing the date in mind, at least evoked a little household sympathy. It was possibly because my blanched appearance could perhaps have been reasonably compared to Dickens' description of Marley's ghost. I was not encumbered with chains, you'll understand, but with items that Dorothy and I had gathered together for our domestic use in addition to all my naval uniform and attendant gear.

At last I managed to restore family relationships to a tentative even keel, got so much needed rest and soon felt sufficiently recovered to report to 798 Squadron. I reckon that neighbours were of the opinion that I had survived a shipwreck!

798 Squadron was at RN Air Station, Peplow, close to Market Drayton in Shropshire — a cold spot in a bleak mid winter.

I journeyed to Market Drayton in the customary unheated carriage and, after recovering the use of my legs, found transport to Peplow. It was cold and uninviting. A new project was afoot. Instructors were now flying in pairs, the pilot being sternly criticised by his passenger on all his control movements in handling the plane. The passenger, in his turn, suffered severe torments when the positions were reversed. The atmosphere was anything but relaxed.

Not surprisingly, I was disenchanted at the prospect of performing this routine and sought to avoid it if at all possible. I found salvation.

As luck would have it an assignment came up. An instructor was needed at HMS *Ringtail*, Burscough in Lancashire to fly with the pilots joining a newly formed Firefly squadron destined for the aircraft carrier *Warrior*. I volunteered, got the job and on 3rd January I was off to Burscough with a petty officer pilot and two Harvard aircraft. Burscough was fairly near to my home in Manchester. The task was pleasant and not arduous. It might well see my naval service through. It did!

It might well have seen me off, or at least seen me concluding my service with a nasty accident and a court martial. It didn't!

The new squadron members were late in reporting and came piecemeal, so that by 17th January I had done but six flights and enjoyed a couple of weekends at home. Unexpectedly on that day, I received notice that the requisite documents being to hand, I might return to Peplow to formalise my demob procedures as soon as I wished. I resolved to do so the very next day.

The eighteenth of January was perishing. Light wispy snow was falling. I arranged that a Harvard be fuelled and reported to Flight Control for clearance. Clearance was refused. There was no immediacy for me to return for demob that day, but I had stubbornly resolved that I was going. Flight Control collectively, about half a dozen of them, told me that the weather was quite unsuitable for flying and that was that. It wasn't. I played my trump card, the self authorising certificate I was awarded on completing my flying instructors course and effectively overruled them.

I told them I was off, at which they adopted a sorrowful mien, said they were pleased to have met me, shook hands with me one by one and doubted if they would renew the acquaintance.

Pilot navigation was straightforward. A pencilled line on the map, an approximate course, having regard to the wind strength and direction, the recognition of any particular landmarks en route and any necessary corrections to the course as one observed them — a piece of cake! My points of reference were the stretches of water on the Cheshire Shropshire border. Very distinct they were.

I got airborne through some snow flurries and gained altitude, aiming to level out at two thousand feet, a desirable height for map reading. The snow flurries exceeded my expectations so that at two thousand feet I could not see the ground. Perforce, I descended to a thousand feet. I could now just see the ground, but at that height the ground goes past at too swift a rate to make for comfortable map reading. I set my approximate course, flew at a low speed and hoped for the best, being confident that my landmarks of meres would be all I wanted to make directional adjustments.

"The best laid plans o' mice an' men gang aft agley". Not half! My plans were absurdly faulty never mind best laid. I had neglected to appreciate that water being frozen and snowed upon virtually disappears as a landmark. I peered from the cockpit seeking the meres. The meres were not there. Where was I? The countryside under snow is singularly featureless. In short, I was lost.

I knew that I had crossed the Manchester Ship Canal and was therefore beyond Runcorn and somewhere above the Cheshire Plain. Apart from that it was guesswork. Unless I could establish my precise position, I was in deep trouble.

My concentrated attention to map reading was to the neglect of the instrument panel. One automatically glances at the airspeed indicator and the altimeter but not so assiduously at the engine instruments. I could scarce believe my eyes! The cylinder head temperature gauge read way below its optimum working temperature. The indicator needle was actually falling. I realised that I must land inside fifteen minutes at most or make some sort of forced landing. *Sic transit gloria* Sadler.

To be flying in foul weather, against specific orders, lost and with a cockpit flap is a singularly unpleasant experience. I felt near disaster and tense as a bowstring. The Harvard flew inexorably on but it would not do so for long.

I had been in many operational sorties and emerged unscathed. This wretched situation was entirely of my own making. It was up to me to emerge from it. I was not in touch with any ground station which might help me in some way. Immediate action was essential, but what?

There was but one possible hope of salvation I could conjure up. It was an old one. I called it 'Bradshaw'. I'd try it. Would it work?

I swung the aircraft round to the east searching for a railway line. Got it — the Manchester to Crewe line. All who have travelled by rail over the years have spent dismal hours waiting at Crewe. No waiting was envisaged on this occasion. Changing course to the south, I flew alongside the line, now down to five hundred feet as the snow thickened, looking out for stations. Crewe came into sight — bear right — Nantwich, Whitchurch, Prees Heath. Now for it. Steer south south east and pray. Mercifully the bearing was true. I shimmered in over the perimeter of the frozen waste that was Peplow. The small control tower was just discernible. Disregarding wind direction or duty runway, I landed, taxied to the Air Watch office and parked alongside the only aircraft on the field, a DH89.

My reporting to the Duty Officer caused a stir. He asked me where the hell I'd come from. I told him. He didn't believe me. I suggested that he phoned Burscough. A call confirmed that what I'd told him was true, but he still found it hard to accept. I might as well have come from outer space.

The De Haviland DH89 outside the office was the naval communications aircraft which operated a daily regular service transporting papers between naval air stations. It had taken off from Peplow, executed one circuit of the airfield and landed. The pitot head was completely frozen up so that it had no airspeed reading.

It was my last naval flight — but there was no flying! I had of course, travelled by rail, but my log book shows Harvard EZ397 Burscough to Peplow, forty minutes and that was all about it.

I was relieved to find myself alive and 'off the hook' albeit somewhat tremulous and marvelling at my good fortune in not paying dearly for my obstinate conceit. Mind you, I still carried it off well.

My demob routine was effected smoothly the next day and I returned home in orthodox public transport — still cold! 'Home' did not really exist. Dorothy and I had to find a place to live, which meant rented accommodation sharing a house with a middle aged spinster who erroneously assumed she'd got a gardener handyman and a housekeeper. There was nowhere else, no properties to rent and none we could afford to buy.

Chapter 17 — Home the Conquering Hero Comes

I could liken my return to the General Post Office to a forced landing. My pupil pilot had regrettably failed to select a suitable landing field and foundered. My landing field was arranged for me. I made an orthodox approach observing official edicts. It might be interesting and instructive to describe how the hero returned from the wars and how good it felt to be back — a job reasonably well done, or so I thought. Had my gliding approach from downwind been in the familiar open cockpit of a Swordfish I might have been cognisant of the stench from the machinations of the GPO Management prepared for returning ex-servicemen.

My welcoming committee comprised an office employee who had, he considered, achieved signal success in being transferred from sorting office to writing duties. He was entitled to wear a suit instead of the drill overall coat effected by the sorting clerks. He asked my name and from which of the services I had been demobilised. Recording my answers he then enquired of the rank to which I had risen, recorded that, then archily enquired what decorations I had been awarded. My reply "none" brought a slightly supercilious expression to his face. I held my peace. The attitude of my interrogator displeased me. I did not warm to the self satisfied wimp. He was of that age that was much too young for the First war and under the 'reserved occupation' category was just too old for the draft in the Second. His anxious concern between '39 and '45 must have been the wear and shine on his trouser seat, mindful of the dearth of clothing coupons. He sat on his arse during standard office hours.

My gorge rising, I thought to smite him and remove the smug expression from his face. I thought to, but didn't.

Instead I signed on the dotted line, which then entitled me to my drill coat, my towel, my tablet of soap, my pencil and the key for my numbered locker.

How good it felt to be back!

The office looked the same, having suffered no obvious wartime damage. Its size exceeded that of a football field. Here, before the war, I had rated well in the top ten for speed and accuracy of sorting. Without any mechanical aids I had on test reached a rate of three thousand eight hundred letters an hour over a measured short period. Hardly any other sorters improved on that.

Naturally I was frustrated and felt cheated being directed back there. Other ex service acquaintances had help in advancing their careers. They were in receipt of greater sums of money in grants that I earned. Stan Thomas went to Oxford, Barringer to Cambridge, Urquhart and Sargent to medical studies, Robin Shirley Smith to architecture school. I could go on. All my close pre war friends in the GPO had lost their lives in the war. Not one of them returned as I did. Their great loss saddened me.

Had there been changes and improvements during my absence? Well, yes and no. Such changes as there were might well have been specifically designed to disadvantage me. Improvements I failed to detect.

Working hours remained the same, so I could not complain. It was shift work — a four week turn round — night work, a late week, Monday to Friday 2.30pm to 10.45pm with Saturday 10.15am to 5.00pm, an early week, 7.00am to 3.00pm, Monday to Saturday inclusive and, finally, a late week including a late Saturday. This was a disaster so far as social life was concerned. You might of course attend a soccer match once a month!

The changes incensed me.

Permanent staff away apart from the seniors, the GPO employed temporary females, some barely competent. In 1946 they were being paid more than I was!

An agreement had been reached by the GPO and the Union of Post Office Workers, to take over the indoor work, that done by Sorting Clerks and Telegraphists who belonged to the Guild of SC&Ts — this whilst we were away playing soldiers. The UPW was massive as compared to the G of SC&T. The postmen were not trained to do our work. Returning SC&Ts were held back from taking 'limited competition' Civil Service examinations until they had instructed postmen to do their jobs. Incumbents helping usurpers to take over at their cost! Candidates from outside the Civil Service meanwhile were eligible to take the 'open' examinations, which we were not allowed to take, more than twelve months ahead of us. For the same standard of exams their pass mark was forty per cent inferior to ours.

Whereas pre war the Customs & Excise examination was open to me without hindrance or barriers, The GPO had now imposed one — not the Civil Service Commissioners, but the GPO. I was now required to hold a good School Certificate or Matriculation before being granted permission to sit.

My reaction to the scurvy tricks of my employer was to fight back. My dander gets up when I am faced with something that 'can't be done'.

My superiors, in the GPO sense only, must have found me to be a determined uncompromising employee who performed his job most efficiently, quite above any possibility of adverse criticism, had scant respect for the harsh, unfriendly and less than competent management and made himself more conversant with the rules than they were.

The GPO had the whip hand in making the rules. In less than six months I had obtained the equivalent of a good School Certificate by dint of putting in an eighteen hour day and my application to sit the C&E exam therefore had to be accepted. In due course, 'due course' meaning that I was suffered to wait whilst I distastefully trained others, I was successful in becoming an Officer of Customs and Excise, which was then a prestigious job.

I seemed to have achieved nothing that had benefited me over the seven years that my life had been disrupted. I was no better off. Possibly I had matured a bit and shaken off the shackles of over possessive parents. Maybe I had learned a thing or two.

My wartime journey could fairly be described as a full circle. So many things came to mind as I mulled over the multifarious memories of my maritime meanderings, that I could fill another volume in relating them. Fear not. That is not my intention.

Enemy Coast Ahead

Wing Commander Guy Gibson, VC, DSO, DFC

ISBN 1-872424-50-3

Content

Enemy Coast Ahead has been regarded as a classic work of aviation history since it was first published in 1946. So popular has it been that it has now been continually in print for nearly 50 years. This new edition will prove to be particularly attractive as the book has not appeared in hard-back for many years and has not previously been illustrated. The Bridge Books edition, the third volume in our aviation classics series, will be illustrated with 70+ black and white photographs showing Gibson, his crews, their aircraft, targets, stations etc. **Many of these photographs have never previously been published** and are drawn from the unequalled collection of the noted RAF historian Chaz Bowyer. In addition to the photographs, this volume will also be **illustrated with a number of specially commissioned pencil drawings** of aircraft and an original painting on the jacket showing Gibson's Lancaster as part of a force carrying out a daylight raid against a target in France. This bright and attractive jacket will be a major selling point of this edition. Both the internal drawings and the jacket painting are by aviation artist Malcolm Kinnear, a member of the American Society of Aviation Artists and they will all be available as limited edition, signed prints which will result in added publicity for the book.

Chaz Bowyer has added **a new introduction** giving a brief outline of Gibson's life outside of the period covered by the book, and has **added numerous footnotes** giving biographical details of many of the individuals mentioned in the text. **A revised and now accurate list of aircrew losses** has been incorporated into this edition.

The Bridge Books *Enemy Coast Ahead* will surely become the definitive edition of this classic book.

Chaz Bowyer

Chaz Bowyer, after completing twenty-six years service in the Royal Air Force, has written over 40 books and is regarded as one of the leading British aviation historians. His magnum opus, *For Valour – the Air VCs* is still in print twenty years after its first publication and is universally acclaimed as the definitive work on the subject. His *History of the RAF* has, to date, sold over 120,000 copies, probably a record for any book on British aviation history.

Hardback, 240pp, illustrated, £19.95

Against the Odds

The Life of Group Captain Lionel Rees, VC

W Alister Williams

Against the Odds is the story of Wales' first air hero and Britain's first official fighter pilot. Lionel Rees was an officer in the regular army when war broke out in 1914 and he transferred to the infant Royal Flying Corps. He went to france with No. 11 Squadron the following year and was awarded the Military Cross. On 1 July 1916, he won the Victoria Cross while commanding No. 32 Squadron on the Western front. He played a role in the very early days of the US Air Force and was one of the founding fathers of the RAF College, Cranwell. During the 1920s he was involved with the Druze tribesmen in Transjordan and, whilst in the Middle East, developed a passionate interest in the archaeology of the Old Testament using aerial photography as a source of data. In 1933, he became the first man to sail solo from Britain to the Bahamas and spent several years sailing amongst the West Indian islands before eventually settling on the Bahamian island of Andros where he married and raised a family. A remarkable individual who was once described as ". . . the bravest man in the world", Rees was truly a person who did everything against the odds.

Softback, 284pp, 36 half-tones, 5 maps. ISBN1-872424-00-7. £9.95

Bridge Books is an independent publishing house specialising in books of Welsh history, military history and aviation history. For a full list of our publications please send a SAE (A5) to:

Bridge Books
61 Park Avenue
Wrexham
LL12 7AW
UK